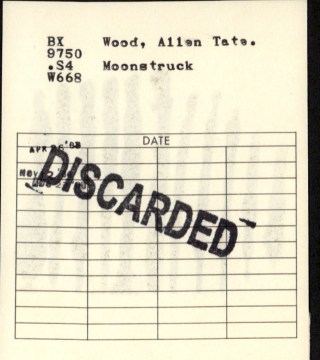

Moonstruck

Moonstruck

A MEMOIR OF MY LIFE IN A CULT

by ALLEN TATE WOOD
with JACK VITEK

WILLIAM MORROW AND COMPANY, INC.
NEW YORK   1979

Library of Congress Cataloging in Publication Data

Wood, Allen Tate.
   Moonstruck.

    1. Wood, Allen Tate.   2. Segye Kidokkyo T'ongil
Sillyŏng Hyŏphoe—Biography. 3. Segye Kidokky
T'ongil Sillyŏng Hyŏphoe—Controversial literature.
4. Moon, Sun Myung.   I. Vitek, Jack, joint author.
II. Title.
BX9750.S4W668   289.9 [B]   79-13035
ISBN 0-688-03512-4

Printed in the United States of America.

First Edition

1   2   3   4   5   6   7   8   9   10

This book is dedicated to my mother and father, who remembered me so well that through them I have been reborn. It is also dedicated to the thousands of young men and women whose uninformed idealism and hunger for righteousness have been turned against them by cynical cult leaders. These parasites wantonly manipulate the openness, generosity, and essential belief in goodness of their young followers. It is my hope that this book in some way may interfere with the emotional and psychological slaughter that is the coin of the realm on the road to Xanadu.

ACKNOWLEDGMENTS

Thanks to Blair, Moira, Doug, Lucianne, Carolyn, Chris, Jack, Amy, and Jim, without whose help *Moonstruck* would not have been possible.

NOTE

Aside from the names of prominent public figures and of those members of the Unification Church who are known to the public, names of all others have been changed to protect their privacy.

Moonstruck

> So much of democratic social theory reaches us
> in the language of "drive," "stimulus," and "re-
> sponse." This is . . . the language of slaves.
>
> —ALLEN TATE
> *The Man of Letters in
> the Modern World*

Prologue

I AM VERY MUCH OF AMERICA. MY FAMILY AND MY LATE
adolescence were in so many aspects typical of the time. Yet
for well over four years I drew succor from a movement alien
—both literally and spiritually—to this land.

My ancestors had the courage, energy and vision to explore.
and settle this land. My grandmother, who is a novelist of
note, makes much of the fact that Meriwether Lewis was her
great-great-granduncle. Having earned a reputation as a
writer's writer, Caroline Gordon is still vital in her eighties
and now, in Mexico, is working every day on her twelfth or
thirteenth novel. Lewis, that early surveyor of America, is
to appear as a character in the second half of her new book.

Grandma twice married and was twice divorced from Allen
Tate, whose namesake I am. Grandpa died recently at seventy-
nine. T. S. Eliot called him "a good poet and a good literary
critic" and praised him for maintaining that "least popular of

political attitudes—that of the sage." Sir Herbert Read called him the most important American critic since Poe.

I was brought up with my mother's tales of how she was dandled on this poet's or that novelist's knee. The Tates twice lived in Paris in the twenties and thirties on Guggenheim grants and, among other things, went to the bicycle races with Hemingway. Grandma refused to associate with Hemingway after he punched a waiter in her presence.

My mother well remembers the summer in Tennessee when she was thirteen and Robert Lowell showed up on their doorstep and declared his intention to study with Tate. On being told there was no room for him, Lowell pitched a tent on the lawn from which he made sorties into Grandpa's spare time. Lowell remained a lifelong admirer of my grandfather.

My father's mother killed herself in 1956, after years of manic-depressive illness. She was descended from people who in my regard loomed like giants from the mists of the Old South.

She was the granddaughter of Governor Alcorn of Mississippi. His was an American rags-to-riches story in the manner of Faulkner. Faulkner patterned the main character in *Absalom, Absalom!* after James Lusk Alcorn, who as a possessionless young man in the second quarter of the 1800's rafted down the Mississippi from Kentucky. He bought twenty of the biggest field slaves—from a fierce tribe from the west coast of Africa that many Southerners despaired of controlling —and worked alongside them in the fields. And he offered them an antique version of profit-sharing: he told them that when he prospered, they would, too.

Faulkner's Sutpen is, after all, fiction, to some extent, but I offer this glimpse of him as an equivalent to my own romantic view of my ancestor:

> So the legend of the wild men came gradually back to town, brought by the men who would ride out to watch what was going on, who began to tell how Sutpen would take stand beside a game trail with the pistols and send the Negroes in to drive the swamp

like a pack of hounds: it was they who told how during that first summer and fall the Negroes did not even have (or did not use) blankets to sleep in, even before the coon-hunter Akers claimed to have walked one of them out of the absolute mud like a sleeping alligator and screamed just in time. The Negroes could speak no English yet and doubtless there were more than Akers who did not know that the language in which they and Sutpen communicated was a sort of French and not some dark and fatal tongue of their own.

Alcorn had twenty-one children, fourteen of them boys who split evenly during the Civil War, according to the legend, with seven fighting for the Union and seven for the Confederacy. He was elected governor in the 1870's, and some Southerners still look down on him as a bit of a copperhead.

My family supplies ample evidence of spiritual hungers. My father, after an episodically mystic childhood and adolescence (in this I am like him), took his Catholicism seriously and insisted that his Episcopalian bride convert. She did. Both lapsed from the Church in the fifties, however, largely over the issue of birth control. And my grandmother, Caroline Gordon, as the story goes, picked up the Bible one day when she couldn't find any good mysteries, read it from cover to cover, and soon converted to Catholicism. Grandpa, from whom she was then divorced, heard about it and wrote her: "We must do this thing together." They were married the second time as Catholics. Grandpa had already developed friendships with some of the important Catholic intellectuals, including the Neo-Thomist philosopher Jacques Maritain.

My father told me he never had any sense of choice. The big things in his life—marriage, children, career—seemed so inevitable to him that they might as well have been dictated. As his father did before him, he went to medical school. He deviated only in his specialty—psychiatry instead of gynecology. My father preached the gospel of the upper-middle-class professional man: Study, which leads to a career, which you stick with through thick and thin, which leads to success, which leads to happiness. It was a path that held not the slightest interest for me.

This is what I'm made of. It's my privilege to think that if I had lived when the country was younger, even in my grandparents' time, I might not have so badly misdirected my youthful energies. That I did misdirect them, I have no doubt now, though I rose in the Unification Church and at one point —when I headed its rabidly anticommunist political arm in Washington—held its second highest rank in the United States. What follows is my contribution to the tradition of confessional literature that comes down to us from Saint Augustine. My chief confession is of a kind of failure of nerve. Beyond that, I seek to understand how and if I might have seized better control of the outside forces that buffeted me this way and that. And, in the manner of confessions, I seek to repair my errors with an offering of belated but all the more vital wisdom. This will be the story of error leading to greater error; the final one, which led me to a limbo I might never have escaped, was to subordinate my will and to surrender my right to make existential decisions.

I see myself not in isolation, but in relationship to my culture and time. What happened to me has happened to others, can happen to still more. Although the numbers of Moon's church have always been smaller than the impression made on the press, I think the suspicious regard in which most Americans instinctively hold Moon is perfectly justified.

Even through the muddled and inflated accounts of Moon's biography I think I can detect evidence of spiritual powers that would at least bring him to the level of the minor mediums he now keeps around him. These are the kind of "spiritualists" most of us regard with skeptical curiosity. There is no doubt they pull off some tricks; no one knows how they do it. But I believe that for some years Moon has not even had these powers of mind reading and healing.

So I arrived in Berkeley, California, in 1969, having left a graceful Southern college existence that seemed like a puerile rehearsal for a life I would never lead. This happened within the same year during which I witnessed from the lower branches of a tree the mindless beating of dissenting youth by Mayor Daley's police at the Chicago convention. The peace movement, that youthful rallying point, had lost its pull for me. My alienation was almost complete. I was cut off from my family. I had broken with my girl friend. In fact, I had no real friends of any kind. I had just slept with the wife of the most decent professor at my college, and that one cut both ways: the established fabric looked pretty seamy and yet I felt a deep guilt for having violated it. (This liberal young couple talked a lot about giving each other freedom to have "affairs." In retrospect I realize they could hardly have been less confused than I.) Having further disoriented myself with the strong hallucinogens of the era, I was headed across the country for India by way of California, in the independent vein of my forefathers, in search of spiritual enlightenment. The only people who showed the slightest interest in me, as I rambled lonely through Los Angeles, were a string of predatory homosexuals. And last but not least, there was my growing sense of failure, which is just a coin-flip from the self-contempt that Moon's mass movement seeks to turn into the self-abnegation so necessary for its prosperity.

Religious insanity is very common in the United States. . . . If ever the faculties of the great majority of mankind were exclusively bent upon the pursuit of material objects, it might be anticipated that an amazing reaction would take place in the souls of some men.

—ALEXIS DE TOCQUEVILLE

IN THE SPRING OF 1968, AS I CLIMBED THE THREE FLIGHTS of stairs to my room, I felt glad that I was no longer compelled to eat lunch with the 799 other Sewanee gentlemen. The greasy institutional food would have been enough to turn any thinking man away from the table. In my room I kept cheese, nuts, and fruit juice. I wanted to be alone; moreover, I wanted to be away from the low-level group psyche which characterized the Kappa Alpha society, which I had just recently dropped out of.

Now I lived here, in a single room in a dorm, amid those whom my fraternity brothers had summarily dismissed as geese, lizards, turkeys and—not to forget their bigotry—Jews. (Sewanee had only one token black.) Individually I had found my brothers at Kappa Alpha nice enough, but together they were something less than nice. That led me to suppose my problem was strictly social. I found them unconscious, meaning I had been sensitized to issues they were oblivious to.

Probably I would take a nap, for with the numbness came

drowsiness. I would cut my afternoon lit class: the siege of Troy would go on without me. If Homer represented the dawning of a consciousness that would later be considered quintessentially Western and civilized—especially here in the South, where the gentlemen of a generation ago still knew their classics—my interests were moving ineluctably eastward. For some months now my sole reading had been a few pages of Rama Krishna each night. I read him not because I had to, not because he was assigned, not because everyone else did, not for good grades, not to become well read in the sense that my mother must have meant, and not even out of the rather idle and disinterested curiosity of the true intellectual, but solely for myself. To say I read him slowly and savoringly would be an understatement. I cracked each word like a sunflower seed for its kernel of meaning.

As for my official studies, I neglected them even more recklessly than during freshman year, which had not been a good year. For one thing, I had flunked biology, which seemed to mean I was not going to be a medical doctor like my father, who had attended Sewanee before me. That was during the early forties when Grandpa Tate, whose daughter my father married, was still here editing *The Sewanee Review*. My roots were deep here, which made it all the more problematical and amazing that I found myself in such conflict with this institution and what it represented. No doubt that was why I still went through the motions—as much as I could, when I could.

I opened my door and threw the morning's mail—a letter from my mother and a copy of *Time*—on my oak desk. I lit the sandalwood incense in its little brass burner on the desk. Then I took the magazine and the envelope with its eccentric straight-up-and-down handwriting to my worn brown velvet armchair. For a moment I gazed out the window, which I had left open this morning. My room was in the back of the Tuckaway Inn—for that was the name of this dorm, formerly a hotel, which overlooked a wooded area. It was April and the trees had just broken out in their small, pale, tender leaves. The perfume of a lovely mountain morning wafted in and then mingled with the sandalwood, which eventually overwhelmed it. That was fine with me; the sandalwood was mine and I wanted to control my world in whatever little way I could.

The magazine was full of pictures of flaming, rioting cities. Martin Luther King had been killed the week before and eleven American cities had burned. Troops ringed the Capitol in Washington. Photographed from a distance Washington looked like a wartime city under air attack: every few blocks various colored plumes of smoke—white, gray and black—climbed to mingle in the ominous haze that loomed over the entire city. The capital, the nation, was convulsed. Yet here the birds still twittered in peace. The reverberation as yet was scarcely perceptible. Oh, there was talk. Talk, talk, talk. But a university was always full of that, harmless academic hot air. After twenty minutes during which I was utterly engrossed, I tossed the magazine on the dusty carpet beside me.

I took a deep breath and gazed out the window. This place in Tennessee, for all its beauty, could not distract me for long from the power of my internal struggles. Then I opened the letter from my mother. We had been carrying on a rather intellectual correspondence. I had argued that social evolution was not possible, that in fact there was little point in looking beyond the individual. I argued from my knowledge of the New England transcendentalists, Emerson and Thoreau, but mostly I based my reasoning on the teachings of Rama Krishna, a religious synthesist who had lived in the nineteenth century in India. My mother, who was far better read than I, wrote to me about de Tocqueville: "Along the way he certainly put his finger on what had formed the national character up to that time. The vast physical resources of the country made the dreams of greed perfectly realizable, made them indeed a national virtue—work hard and you will certainly be rewarded with wealth, if not in the town where you were born, then further west." I read through the letter, dimly conscious that its concerns seemed peripheral to my own.

I went over to the desk and tossed the letter into a drawer with the other letters from my large family, including many from my father. These were exhortations to study hard, at least the early ones were. When my grades made it clear that I was not studying hard, these letters changed. What was I going to do, my father asked continually, so constantly that it became a form of nagging. There was even a sense of panic in these letters. Obviously my father thought that any activity that did not dovetail with the purpose of getting ahead was a waste of energy. My father was not the type to tell me to lose myself in the mysteries and ecstasies of philosophy or literature, to get a liberal education and then decide what I wanted to do. Certainly he was not going to tell me to take a year off and work as a deckhand on a tramp steamer, or some such adventurous and impractical thing. At any rate, there was a war on. I would lose my student deferment and get drafted for sure.

I kicked off my shoes and flopped on the rumpled bed. I burrowed into the pillow, blocking out the light. Tonight I would no doubt sit around and smoke pot with some of the others who were disaffected from the traditions of this conservative school. Sometimes we sniffed amyl nitrate and once we had taken blue morning-glory seeds, which we ground up and put in capsules. A couple of times we had stolen ether from the lab and had taken it out on the mountainside, where we snuffled it in a white wool athletic sock to lose all but a glimmer of consciousness as we rolled down the mountainside. For six seconds I was an astral traveler strapped to the back of a mote of dust, being sucked into a huge celestial furnace.

I used drugs for two reasons: I believed that they might lead me to spiritual truths (I well remembered my father's vivid descriptions of his archetypal journeys on LSD, to which he submitted himself as part of a clinical experiment), and

I was subject to waves of desire for obliteration of my personal history. The desire for knowledge on one hand, and for self-destruction on the other, marked a whole generation.

In the spring of 1968, in addition to reading the works of Swami Paramahansa Yogananda, I read *The Divine Comedy*, studied Russian history, and acted in a school production of *King Lear*. I was cast in the role of Edmund. We rehearsed from February until late April, and while I couldn't seem to pull myself together for my studies, I learned my part well.

The night of our last performance there was a cast party at the home of the director. There was a wonderful electricity in the air that night. I was exhilarated by the admiration of my fellow students and the other actors; playing the part of another person had given me a new perspective and had lifted me out of my introspective torpor.

At the party everyone stood around drinking beer and wine. I had a long talk with John Bessin in the kitchen. He was my favorite professor at Sewanee—a rumpled, tweedy figure, wearing khakis and loafers, and a loosened tie. Bessin was a big man with small hands and feet. Although he was not muscular, he gave a sense of contained power.

Just over his shoulder, in the dining room, where the furniture had been moved against the wall and the record player brought in, I could see John's wife, Margaret, dancing with an undergrad with a moustache. When I had arrived at Sewanee as a freshman last year, scarcely a single moustache, sideburn or beard had been evident among the eight hundred students. Now about a quarter of them wore some kind of facial hair, and only the sparseness of my own whiskers kept me from joining them. Dionne Warwick was singing "Do You Know the Way to San Jose?"

Margaret looked that night the way she had looked the first night I met her, wearing a skirt and sweater, dancing with energetic abandon. Her natural warmth communicated itself unforgettably. All of us who were friendly with John and Margaret were in love with Margaret. She knew and John knew, and we knew that they knew, and it was a joke and a kindness, and it created a delicious tension. At twenty-eight she was nearer our age than his. Had Sewanee been co-ed, perhaps she would not have assumed such an important role for us.

While most of the professors at Sewanee were dry, remote souls who gave the impression that all they wanted to hear from the students were their own words echoing back at them at exam time, John also wanted to listen. Many students were drawn to him because he was unaffected, and he refused to accept or perpetuate the class difference between students and teachers. He made it clear that he had once been in our place, though he had not gone to Sewanee himself. He had the gift of recognizing that a deep understanding of books and ideas was only possible through an identification with the problems, situations, and characters contained in those books.

A kind of honesty was manifest in John in his insistence that a personal commitment to intellectual pursuits take precedence over the enshrined, time-honored academic approach. John made it look like it could be fun. On those evenings when we informally gathered to discuss art, literature and politics, he offered us a doctrine as sincere as it was academic, for it came straight from Shakespeare and Restoration drama. He suggested that a finer sensibility was slow to come to itself, took growing pains, and if it seemed at first more awkward than the sensibility of those with such clear and smooth-running goals, it would ultimately be discovered to be infinitely more valuable, just as the other would be found limited and mean-spirited. After all, most of Sewanee's graduates would find their place in the world of commerce. They would not end up artists or scientists or even English professors.

Nor were our impulses to be mistrusted. Thus he offered us also a release from the American Puritanism that still survived in a virulent fundamentalist form in the South: what was good was what felt bad. On the contrary, we of John's circle maintained, impulse was the handmaiden of inspiration, divine or poetic, and the gateway to the path of truth. This included one kind of impulse that very much concerned us, too—sexual impulse. Margaret would be there, sitting on the floor, and this would be one of the times when everyone would take a few puffs of a passing joint. John was open-minded, but he would never be a pothead. There, with the music playing in the background—Dylan, Donovan or the Mothers of Invention—he once explained to us his rather Blakean doctrine of open marriage. Better to strangle infants in their cribs than to harbor secret and unacted desires, he propounded, and Margaret nodded. He was not his wife's jailor, nor was she his. They could go to bed with whomever they pleased, he said and she nodded, provided they were open and honest and decent about it. Adultery was as outmoded as sin. Their love was a higher thing of the spirit that the flesh could not sully.

Out in the kitchen I swallowed the last of a beer, clanged the can into a garbage bag already half full of empties and reached for the refrigerator door handle.

"So John, what did you think of the play?" I said.

"Lear is rather unwieldy, but I have to admit, I like it when the bad guy is a handsome devil."

I offered him a beer, which he refused.

"I'm beat. I think I'm going to hit the hay, Allen."

"Don't leave, man. Pete and Steve are coming over from the Kappa Sig house in a while. I know Pete wanted to see you."

"Tell him I'll talk to him when we play touch football with the kids tomorrow. Take it easy . . ."

"Good night, John."

Indeed, John did look tired. Margaret had not been able to buffer him from all the pressures of his life as a teacher, husband and father.

Over his shoulder I could still see Margaret dancing; she looked small, seen framed in the doorway, like a genie from a bottle. Margaret the searcher. How upset she had been that night last week after Martin Luther King had been murdered. Margaret so full of passion. Once she had told me she wished she could love all men.

Out in the living room I overheard Richard Colgate, one of the heavies, indeed one of the dinosaurs, since he had been chairman of the English department since the forties, tell Chuck Martin and Bill Galen that our production of *Lear* was the best he had ever seen at Sewanee. Well now, that was saying something. Not that this made the slightest impression on those two, who had nothing to do with the production and who were moreover—one a professor and one a student— young men obsessed with radical issues. Colgate was just moving on, possibly sensing in what low regard he was held by them.

I stepped into the spot he vacated, keeping the conversational triangle complete. Martin rolled his head in his strange excitable way and focused his big brown pop-eyes on me. He held a cup of wine in his hand, but it wasn't the alcohol. This twenty-seven-year-old Ph.D. in Russian studies and professed Communist was always wound up, in or out of the classroom.

"Columbia was just the beginning," he said, and Bill and I nodded. Bill headed SDS at Sewanee, and I was a member. Indeed the Columbia demonstration in which the cops' behavior had "radicalized" so many students—radicalized them with billy sticks, fists, and steel-shod feet—had soon been followed by a student revolt at Howard University in Washington. The year was young, but already it promised to be the most eventful one I had lived through. Already McCarthy had registered his stunning success in the New Hampshire primary and last month Johnson had stopped the bombing in Vietnam—or had said he had—a transparent effort to ambush McCarthy's quiet but determined campaign. And the polls showed that the American population was reaching the point of absolute polarization on the Vietnam war—half for, and half against.

But Bill allowed that he had reservations about how large

a role a conservative, traditional backwater institution like Sewanee might play in such a new beginning. He well knew that besides the two of us there were no more than eight other SDS members on campus.

"Talk about the plantation mentality. This is where it was invented," he said.

But Martin's optimism was not to be dampened, not even by the wine he slopped on his shoes as he made a sweeping gesture and quoted H. Rap Brown's recent statement at Cambridge, Maryland: "Violence is as American as apple pie." This odd, tall, scruffy, skinny man with the premature potbelly could soar in the lecture hall, but socially he was as clumsy as an albatross on foot. He looked down at the wine on his shoes, searched his pockets for a handkerchief that wasn't there and then proceeded to stand alternately on either foot and wipe each shoe on the back of the other pants leg.

Then, rolling his eyes around the room, he took a sip, probably his first since someone had stuck the cup of wine in his hand. He was the picture of a man obsessed and of the new emerging breed of radical professor. What a strange position he found himself in, with the passions of a student and the position of a professor. He had buckled down, had gotten the big degree and then had found that the very part of himself he had strangled in that library carrel now craved expression. Whatever rite of passage most of these paunchier professors had gone through that made them think they held superior wisdom, Martin had not crossed the line. Not that he wasn't a good teacher. In his Socratic way he was far better than they. Perhaps it was just that it had happened so fast. He was still only twenty-seven. If he had been promoted into management, his heart still beat to the tune of trade unionism.

And so he proceeded to counsel Galen.

"What you need is an issue. They had an issue at Columbia."

"Oh, we've got our issue. Those fucking stained-glass windows." Bill and I had discussed this before. It was in many ways a better issue. It seemed to us absolutely unconscionable that the university should pay $25,000 apiece for a dozen stained-glass windows in the chapel and refuse to raise the wages of the black near-slaves in the kitchen above the legal minimum.

But for once I kept my opinions to myself. For one thing, I had remembered that paper I was supposed to be doing for Martin. He was teaching a course called Idealism and Realism Throughout History and I was writing a paper on revolutionary messianism. It was soon due and I'd hardly gotten past the title.

Martin fixed me with his strange abstract gaze.

"What about you, Wood? What do you think? You're being mighty quiet tonight."

His voice contained the firm edge of authority. Was this Martin the friend and radical, or Martin the young professor? The conflicts of his role, real or not, sometimes boggled me. Against the system or not, Martin still graded papers and exams and turned them in to the registrar.

I shrugged and smiled my smile of a Shakespearean villain. I backed away. And by way of explanation I shook the empty beer can I held.

"Back in a minute," I said, conscious that I was already a little drunk.

The tenor of things changed very quickly as soon as the first joint was passed around furtively in a downstairs bedroom. (Some of the heavies were still lurking about.) Maybe it was that mysterious arrangement of my perceptions, but it seemed to me that the party was also thinning out to the more desperate souls. Within a quarter of an hour I was picking over the remains of the buffet table, dry roast beef, ham curled and darkened, soggy crackers and limp slices of cheese—never better than with a marijuana appetite. I was rolling a slice of ham around a hunk of cheese when I looked up and saw Margaret across the table.

"Why, you've been smoking, Allen."

I nodded and smiled sheepishly, my cheeks lumpy with crammed food.

"Where?"

I told her to wait there until I got back with a joint. When I did we smoked the whole thing standing in a shadowy corner. As we exhaled the last puff I asked her to dance. From then on my memory of the rest of the evening was of Margaret's luminous presence, never more than three feet away. We faced one another, our gazes interlocked as we danced those dances that permitted only a modicum of body contact. John had left on foot for their house, not many blocks away, leaving their car for Margaret. Two hours later the party was over, except for me, Margaret and the Robertsons, whose house this was. Then the Robertsons went to bed.

We walked outside. Now the mountain air was cutting cool. We took off all our clothes anyway. The morning dew was on the grass. This was nature, this was spring, this was poetry. The buds were on the trees. The Robertsons' flower garden was coming up. The dawn and the twittering birds were not far away. Our coupling was quick and urgent. We dressed carelessly, went inside, poured more wine, and Margaret lay the golden bowl of her head in my lap. And then, at our greater leisure, as if to prove our act was not simple passion or bad judgment, we made love again, this time in the Robertsons' guest room.

Margaret drove me back to my dorm, where I fell blissfully asleep. It was not until I woke up that the guilt hit me. Nothing, certainly not all those evenings of worldly conversation at the Bessins', had prepared me for what I felt. With the tension of my unfulfilled sexual desires released, I was left with the certain feeling that I had severed my relationship with one of the most important males in my undergraduate life.

I looked around the nearly deserted dining hall. I looked at my empty plate and wondered what I had eaten. We had come back after my speech on the steps of the burned-down

ROTC building and were among the last served. Yes, I remembered now. Salisbury steak, mashed potatoes and gravy and a shredded carrot salad in gelatin. Not so hard to forget. It was my unfortunate nature to eat compulsively when I was upset and I knew this was going to pay off someday in a terrible weight problem.

They were all telling me—Martin, Galen, Gordon, McKay—that my speech had been good. Martin had given his talk drawn largely from his knowledge of theoretical Marxism and full of his characteristic nervous, jerky movements. Then McKay, a French professor, had rambled on in a nice scholarly way on the virtues of pacifism.

I reached for the shining metal coffeepot that Robie had set on the table. Robie was the student waiter, a big, blond mountain boy here on a football scholarship. He was about six-four, well over two hundred pounds, a gentle, easygoing good ole boy, one of the many of his type who saw Sewanee as the road up and out to better things. He was hardworking and obedient, here in the dining hall, out on the turf or in the classroom. I liked him and ordinarily we spoke. But today he had silently avoided my eyes. Although he could not have heard what I said this noon hour of this April 24, the day of the first national student strike for peace, he had no doubt drawn his conclusions from the company I was keeping.

I suppose I had been chosen to speak because I was one of the most cleaned-up members of the SDS. Others had better radical credentials. Someone had set fire to the ROTC building a few weeks ago, and it had burned to the ground. It must have been a personal act of one individual student, but naturally SDS fell under suspicion. It may even have been one of our boys. Nobody seemed to know who had done it. But it had not derived from SDS policy. So far our policy was all talk, and judging from the reaction today, that was enough.

I took a sip of tepid coffee. I still felt separated from my senses. Some of the jocks in the back had thrown eggs at me in long arcs. They had been easy enough to dodge, but the raw hostility had unsettled me.

Galen, I could see, was really pleased. All week now he had been making noises as if he wanted me to be the one to take the torch of leadership from him, to head SDS next year. That was certainly okay with our radical mentor, Martin, who was pressing me to become a communist. Of course, you didn't get a card; "becoming" a communist was entirely an act of self-declaration. While being a communist at Sewanee was tempting because it was so deliciously diabolical, I simply wasn't ready. I had learned much from Martin and his Russian history course, but he was still only one of several influences—among them Bessin, who was sort of a cultural mentor and not much involved in active politics. I was resisting but not denying Martin's and Galen's pressures, trying to hold to what felt right for me.

Today I had taken another giant step away from authority and toward what I welcomed as a new identity. There on the concrete steps that had survived the fire and in front of a crowd of several hundred—it was noon and we were near the dining hall—I gave my speech, extemporaneously. I said that the United States had no right to be in Vietnam. I said that we were interfering in a civil war and that there had been no communist aggression in Vietnam. I said that our cloak of democracy was a pretense and that it concealed our real imperialistic interests, which among other things included raw materials from Third World countries. I spoke of the military/industrial complex and how the military brass and the corporations were in cahoots. Furthermore, I said, we should turn our energy inward; our cities were in turmoil, the country was not yet integrated. And then, amazing myself that I was able to be articulate under these circumstances, I posed some passionate questions. How, I asked, were these students at this conservative American Episcopalian school able to go on logging their thirty-five compulsory chapels per semester, their seven required Sunday services, how were they able to think of themselves as Christians, to go on brushing their teeth, getting drunk, going to classes and preparing themselves for their careers as doctors and lawyers, as insurance men, little Southern politicians and used-car salesmen, how could they go on with all this knowing that they or the guy to the left or right of them was soon going to be sent to Southeast Asia to murder innocent peasants?

These ideas, which I had garnered from Martin, from the radical circle here, from the speeches of Martin Luther King and Eugene McCarthy as reported in the press, from the underground newspapers and *Ramparts* magazine and sometimes even from the editorials in *The New York Times*—these ideas were reviled.

We were practically the last people to leave Gaylord Hall that day. We were keeping Robie, who was sprawled and loitering at a nearby empty table, his cropped head lowered. As I passed he spoke.

"Why don't you go back to Russia!" he exclaimed rather than asked.

At first I thought it was a joke. But no, it wasn't. That guttural snarl was real. Then I thought he was talking to Martin. But when I turned to look back Robie's eyes bored into mine. And his ruddy blond complexion was clouded, blotched. Robie's blood was up; this steamroller of a youth was absolutely enraged.

Perhaps my main achievement that year was my growing sense of being a political presence on campus. Academically I hadn't done much. When the final accounting rolled around my grades were not anything to be proud of: D's in Shakespeare, French and Dante, C in Spanish and B in Martin's Russian history course. I could hardly scrape any lower and still get by. In June, the month of Robert Kennedy's assassination, I went home to face the music. At first I was greeted at the big house on Hodge Road in Princeton, where the family had lived since 1954, with a reserved, maybe even a tolerant silence. But I would soon discover that my parents' fuse was only hanging fire.

Meanwhile, the bright spot was that my mother, previously almost completely apolitical, had become politicized, if not radicalized, on the issue of the war. My mother, who had maybe voted for two presidents in her whole life, was now New Jersey fund-raiser for Gene McCarthy. In this, the era of the generation gap, and on this, the issue of the war that so often split the older and the younger, it was a delight and a luxury to see eye to eye with my mother.

What had done it, of course, was the fact that she now had two draft-age sons, me and my older brother Pete, who was now undergoing Peace Corps training. Certainly no political issue had been able to touch my parents previously. Until this time, they had been largely apolitical. My mother's energies had been consumed in raising four active children, and my father had been engrossed in his studies as a medical student and psychiatric resident, and later in establishing his psychiatric practice as director of the Carrier Clinic. But now my mother wondered about her national identity, America, and its politics, as never before. This was the genesis of her current readings in de Tocqueville. What McCarthy was discovering—and his campaign was now being described both as surprising and as a groundswell—was that there were many more like her. And unlike the radical students, these people were enfranchised and they had money. That summer my mother—with her social charm and contacts—raised about $800,000 for McCarthy.

I worked for her, without pay, running errands, driving a carful of McCarthy literature to a nearby town, canvassing for the candidate's two New Jersey speeches, helping with mailings, licking stamps, and doing whatever else seemed to need doing in the downtown office on Nassau Street. In that regard the summer was shaping up as torpid and easygoing. I often indulged my now well-established vice of sleeping late.

McCarthy was a great candidate as far as I was concerned. I was delighted that he was a poet, that he had spent a year in a Benedictine monastery. He was a Catholic, of course, as we, the Woods, were Catholics, not that anyone in the family went to Mass anymore. McCarthy had even been a friend of my grandparents, Allen Tate and Caroline Gordon, when Grandpa was on the faculty of the University of Minnesota in the early fifties.

That summer I fell in love with Florence Battle. We had known each other since we were tiny children, had played together when I was five and she was three. Now I was twenty-one and she was nineteen, and we went to bed together. It was a meeting of minds and bodies and a wonderful thing for both of us, yet fraught with problems that seemed insurmountable. It was for both of us our first adult, or semi-adult affair (Margaret and such scuffles didn't count), meaning that at last we felt we could take what the law had already given us: we were free and past the age of consent. Yet in another way we were still children. I was still economically dependent on my parents and lived at home, as did Flo. She was working for the summer at Firestone Library on the Princeton campus, having just finished her freshman year at Boston University, where she had gotten her first dose of sheer feminine competition—in grades, clothes, men, sex, looks, everything.

So as often as not when I finally awoke it would be nearly time for lunch. I would walk down to meet Flo at the campus green in front of Nassau Hall, where we would buy fancy groceries and fruit at the German deli across the street and eat and lie on the grass with the hippie element.

Flo and I still looked straight. I dressed sloppily but somehow conventionally, largely, I suppose, out of neglect. There was nothing much about my aura that would lead a cop to itch for a good drug bust. And Flo even looked like a lady, wearing dress-up, silky things to her job. She was a petite but athletic girl of about five-two and one hundred five pounds. She had black hair, freckles, an oval face.

But we felt like weirdos. I was now particularly conscious of going in a different direction from so many of my Princeton friends, many of whom I had known for years, through high school. Most of us had gone away for school, as I did to the Webb School in Belbuckle, Tennessee. Then, as now, during summers we would meet here and there in beautiful Princeton houses, in basement rec rooms, at swimming pools (like our own on Hodge Road), outside at garden parties. Now so many of these young men—and by no means were all of them in McCarthy's ranks—seemed headed from their elite private colleges on to careers in banking, university teaching, on Wall Street, to the professions and the easeful well-to-do lives of our parents.

Flo could spend hours worrying over things I would make up my mind about in a minute. She would wonder, was Johnson really such a villain, McCarthy such a shining knight? Was it really as simple as all that? And sex, she would ask, tightening the vise on the lingering, free-floating guilt that I must admit I could not entirely shake myself, was it really all right for us to lounge around and make love, as we would when we got the chance, three times a day? Our jobs were certainly a small impediment.

"What are you going to do with your life, Allen?" she asked one day, lying there on the grass and finishing up a plastic dish of deli potato salad.

I was sensitive on this issue. I avoided her green eyes.

"Do you think you can just tread water like this all your life?" she asked.

I told her I had this terrible feeling that my childhood, our childhood, was over. Except that where adulthood, where the future should be, I just saw a great blank. Nothing.

I was frightened by such questioning. I felt Flo was attacking me. I took the questions to heart. I also knew that what

Flo was reminding me of was that if *I* didn't have a future, what future did *we* have? I had no idea of the long perspective; I had no life plan; the world that loomed before my mind's eye was a world I really had no desire to take part in. My fear of failing in the dog-eat-dog world of the marketplace somehow made her know that she would have to cast her lot apart from mine. Our love could not be fed by any realistic hopes or dreams of the future.

We smoked a lot of dope that summer and one way or another would end up in Flo's room at the top of the stairs on the second floor of her home. After making love we would lie there on her bed, a huge, high old single, staring at the picture of the Buddhist female deity on her wall. Both of us had just finished reading Hesse's *Siddhartha*. As likely as not, we would have just returned from a party. Eventually Flo would fall asleep on the bed, and sometimes I would let myself go to sleep beside her. Then I would wake up in the early morning and sneak home. But usually I tucked her in and walked the few blocks to Hodge Road.

Flo's parents respected our privacy. She even had her own bathroom. And what did they suppose we were doing up there? My parents well knew, and so I was not allowed to bring Flo to my room at home. My parents said it would be a bad influence on my two younger sisters, Amy, who was eleven, and Caroline, sixteen.

Flo's father, a concert violinist and composer of international repute, although terribly absorbed in his career, even in old age, was the member of her family toward whom she looked with the greatest faith and trust. Her mother, a Catholic pacifist, seemed to approve of me more than my own parents did.

My parents, at best, were whipsawing me. My mother, for her part, sensed my alienation and hoped that my work with the McCarthy people would stimulate me to do something, to, for God's sake, get involved. Maybe I would go on and major in political science and even get through college. Sometimes I was lulled into thinking that my parents had been forced to shelve the question of Allen's dubious future.

But really it was not possible, especially with my father. Now and then I could sense in him the fury, the fear, the panic that finally manifested itself that night when I returned from Flo and found my parents sitting in the backyard with drinks in their hands. The evening had ended early for all of us. It was about ten-thirty. They had just said good-bye to guests who had come for dinner, drinks and a dip in the pool. They were still wearing their bathing suits under terrycloth robes. They had drunk a lot, and no doubt alcohol had a lot to do with unleashing this storm upon me.

My father started it. He was a big man, a powerful man really, in many respects. He had been a boxer in college. He was tall, forceful, intelligent, confident, broad-shouldered and fit. Behind him was the backyard, over which he had labored for fourteen years. Planted on the borders of his little domain were the magnolia, the white pines, the hemlock and white birch, and the bamboo which flourished here. Here in the backyard, he could create a visible order by the sweat of his brow; in his children, little order could he find.

"What are you doing, Allen?"

I didn't answer.

"I'll tell you what you're doing. Nothing!" When my father was drinking, his Tennessee drawl became more pronounced.

"You've never done anything, Allen. You *are* a failure. You always *have been* a failure. You're always *going to be* a failure."

More than the words themselves—their meaning was slow to sink in—it was his sudden vehemence that shocked me. I looked to my mother. With a curiously numb-handed gesture she brushed a lock of gray-blonde hair from her forehead, the Tate forehead that she shared with me and my grandfather alike. Her pale greenish eyes avoided mine. Her mouth tightened. She shook her head and took a sip of her drink. She was on my father's side. Everybody was going to hop Allen.

My father took another swig on his drink, a martini. He was burning the stuff like airplane fuel. I'd seen him loaded many a time on this, his favored and yet worst drink. Being a psychiatrist he understood the application of mood-altering drugs like alcohol. My parents' social circle ran on alcohol.

Surely in all these people there was some pain or rage undealt with, perhaps remaining even totally unconscious, that required numbing. But I was reminded, looking at my father with blood in his eye, that whatever the pain, the rage, the degree of the drinking, he let nothing, but nothing interfere with his work. The first principle of his life was his career. Work had been and still was his very salvation. And that was the one thing I was not doing. I sensed the complex and alarming medley of emotions that jangled my father as he contemplated me.

My mother jumped in to enumerate some of my latest sins, which ranged from sleeping late to not getting the office mail out on time. Then while my mother sipped, my father went over my poor grades. I felt like a drunk in an alley getting zapped by two thugs.

"For God's sake, Allen, what do you believe in?"

It was the crescendo. His glass was empty. My father got up and loomed over me, glowering. So ultimately it was a religious issue. I remembered a somewhat calmer time when my father had asked me what I believed in. I had tried to explain then about my reading of the yogis.

I couldn't make myself think of an answer to this question. I could find in myself no real justification for my existence. Sometimes it seemed to me that I was a kind of extra body, albeit an inferior one, that had been created to house the broken aspects of my father's personality. As I looked into his flashing eyes I saw myself sitting at the dining-room table for Sunday lunch, with my mother and father, my elder brother

Pete and my little sister Caroline. I had just seen *Twenty Thousand Leagues Under the Sea*, and at age seven I was full to the bursting point with enthusiasm for Captain Nemo, the *Nautilus*, and the giant squid. I began to tell my father, at whose right hand I sat, about the movie. Within the space of about three minutes, he corrected my grammar at such painful length, that by the end I no longer had a story to tell —in fact there was no longer anything at all inside me.

Looking at him now, I did not dare be flippant.

"It's not that bad, Dad. The picture isn't that dark. I'm not going down the tubes. Don't worry. I'm just confused. I don't like Sewanee, either. Maybe it would be better if I could go somewhere else. I've been thinking, remember how Pete went out West and pulled himself together? Maybe I could transfer to a more cosmopolitan campus. Maybe I could go to NYU or somewhere like that."

It was my mother who answered: "No, you don't deserve that. You must make a success of Sewanee. And besides, you know your grades are abysmal. They'll never take you."

In mid-July Flo and I drove up to hear McCarthy speak at Madison Square Garden. It was a good speech, as I always thought McCarthy's were. If he lacked the fire that some people called charisma, to me he had always had a cooler and finer appeal. But now something was lacking, something harder to perceive and more subtle than the wisps of smoke from the damping of a fire. Flo sensed it, too.

"What do you think it is?" I asked as I wove around the turnpike cloverleaf and off through the rich New Jersey farmland in my parents' car. Not an hour out of the teeming city crowds, we were already back in another world.

"I think it's when Bobby Kennedy got killed. Somehow I think that took something out of him."

"But how? Bobby was rotten to him. First of all, he didn't have the courage to test the water himself. Then after Gene did, he came in. Do you know what the Kennedy people did at Martin Luther King's funeral? They locked Gene in the bathroom so Bobby could get in all the pictures. And now the Kennedy people won't even help him. God, all that waste. How I hate it. People like Sorenson . . ."

Later I came to agree with Flo, even if I never fully could articulate why. Was it that McCarthy never forgave the American people for turning away from him in such droves after a wealthier, more opportunistic and vulgarly glamorous candidate stole his issue? McCarthy, I suspected, was enough of a poet and a black Irishman to do that, even against his own self-interest. More and more, when I had the opportunity to study him, I thought I could see his lip curl with just a perceptible tinge of distaste or even disgust.

I survived my parents' onslaught beside the pool that night the same way I was surviving everything. By shelving it. And they buried the issue, too. I was left, however, with a heightened sense of living on a fault line. I would never forget that glimpse of their anger, the magnitude of which had shaken me.

So the summer wore on peacefully until, in late August, I drove to Chicago with my pal Norbert to attend the Democratic National Convention, where my mother would soon arrive to serve in the New Jersey delegation. When on a Friday evening we sighted the granaries on the outskirts of this, the great breadbasket of the Midwest prairies, a cool wind was blowing off Lake Michigan. More than just ordinary big-city tension was in the air as we moved into the more congested lanes. On roadside billboards we read the message, scrawled crudely in red paint: "Welcome to Prague." Referring, of course, to the events of just a few days before when Russian tanks had rolled into the Czech capital to fasten the leash of totalitarianism on Dubcek's wandering regime.

Nevertheless, I took an instant liking to Chicago. We had a lovely weekend around the city, returning to sleep on the floor in sleeping bags with many other McCarthy workers in a big house someone had loaned out. Chicago seemed to me a lovely lakeside city, full of beautiful parks, with many museums. There were lots of long-legged Midwestern blondes in the pink of corn-fed health, too, much to the delight of Norbert, who fancied himself a womanizer. Norbie, whose father was a honcho in a big jeans company, had just finished his junior year at Penn, where he was majoring in American studies. He was a bright fellow, who sometimes in all his intensity seemed, mainly because of his two big, white front teeth, like a rabbit or a chipmunk.

By Sunday, when my mother arrived, we'd gotten the lay of the city. She took a room in the Conrad Hilton, where McCarthy had his headquarters on the eleventh floor.

Monday evening Norbie and I came upon Norman Mailer and Robert Lowell waiting for an elevator. Lowell was a tall, disheveled, round-shouldered man who wore a rumpled light jacket and baggy dark slacks and loafers. He smoked nervously and surely would have been more at home on a campus than here in the center of the gathering storm. The broader, shaggier Mailer looked electric, alert, and later, of course, he would put down his idiosyncratic account of the convention in a book. I wondered, should I speak to Lowell, since he was my grandfather's most publicly successful student. Before I could overcome my shyness the elevator arrived and they were gone. They had been laughing. I caught only an echo and a whiff of Lowell's cigarette as we walked past.

On Monday night my mother's friend, Mrs. Martindell, had a dream that McCarthy won the nomination. By Tuesday it was perfectly clear the fix was in. The Daley forces were in complete control. Most of the time the McCarthy people couldn't even get on the convention floor. And judging from the working-class people I encountered—cab drivers, waiters, bellhops and so on—most of America seemed to be right behind Daley. They couldn't wait to sputter out their opinions. The hippies and the Yippies, who had entered the city in such great and unruly force, and all that was identified with McCarthy and the antiwar movement, whether it was outright treason, free love, nudity, long hair, patched jeans, freedom from the drudgery of low-level bad-paying jobs, drugs, bralessness, middle-aged pinkos, a meddlesome press, softness on communism, or just plain carefree youth—all this left Daley's people inarticulate with rage.

Because I was working for the New Jersey delegation, I had floor privileges. Such privileges were moot, though, since even the delegates were having trouble getting into the convention hall. So Tuesday afternoon Norbie and I thought we would just walk around. Although the atmosphere was ugly and there had been many flare-ups, the violence had not yet really begun.

Around two-thirty that afternoon we walked to a demonstration just in the last stages of getting mopped up. Those who weren't getting carted off by the police were hotfooting it away. The fighting was over and the police were in secure possession: Grant Park, which was right across Michigan Avenue from the Hilton, was mobbed with cops wearing their dark-blue city uniforms. The Chicago police did not wear special riot clothes, except for their robin's-egg-blue helmets. The acrid smell of tear gas burned our nostrils.

When we tried to cross the street back to the hotel, the police blocked our way. So we had to walk way off course to leave the area. The streets and sidewalks around the convention hall for several blocks had a sort of crowded, excited, milling circus atmosphere, what with the news media being all around, often set up in trailers, and all the various groups that felt they had something to say or do or show, hanging around. Drifting almost aimlessly as we were, it wasn't surprising when we bumped into another big demonstration, this one a long snaking line of black people being led by a cart drawn by two mules.

It was the Poor People's delegation, which had lately lived in their shantytown on the Mall in the nation's capital— Resurrection City, as King had named it. King had also named the mules Stennis and Eastland, I recalled, after the two

Southern senators, and they had often appeared in the news media as King had begun his sweep through the South in the spring which he hadn't lived to see ripen into this summer, preaching and drumming up a corps of rural blacks he would take to camp on the nation's doorstep. At last the Poor People were forcibly evicted from Resurrection City, with scarcely a public outcry, not even a convincing enough shriek from their assured allies. Who could doubt that Johnson pulled the strings in Washington? Mayor Washington had to be his puppet, answerable to no electorate, personally appointed by the President. Could it be that the police action on the Mall, followed by a quick sweep with tear gas up 14th Street and into the black ghetto into which the shanty dwellers had fled, was a rehearsal for Chicago? As Mailer himself would say in his book, the nation, everyone, even the liberals, seemed to be tired of black people, of their constant nagging presence, their incessant demands.

As we walked with the group, about fifteen cops on motorcycles swept down the street and took their place at the head of the column. No doubt these people did not have a permit for a demonstration. Permits were another game that had been perfected in Washington. After all, Resurrection City had been leveled after the permit had expired. Now, no more than Daley's forces were letting peace creeps on the convention-hall floor were his police giving permits to demonstrators. No, not at all.

Yet it seemed as if this march were somehow sanctioned by the police, at least so far. So we stayed. When we got in front of the Hilton some guy with a bullhorn popped up and told everyone to sit down, that was cool. We obeyed. Then, as we watched with growing alarm, about two hundred fifty cops came down Balboa Avenue and as many more from down the other side. A bunch of them about five or six deep and sixty wide formed up along Michigan Avenue. I noticed that those in front were mostly officers.

Then, without a word, without any swearing, without

provocation, the cops who were lined up along Michigan Avenue drew canisters of mace and began spraying. At the same time they waded into the silent, seated, peaceful demonstrators swinging their clubs. A great screeching began, and Norbie and I, who were in the front row, leaped up. We turned and ran, locking arms, to get to the rear. We were moving with the police and ahead of them, and we literally walked on people to get away from them. My sole thought was for my own preservation. By the time I came out of that squirming Dantesque hell of bodies, I had lost Norbie.

I ran into Grant Park. I grabbed the lower branches of a likely-looking tree and heaved myself up. Then I climbed, high. Soon the area beneath me was seething, too, as the cops drove the crowd before them. Someone else, a man with a camera, climbed into the lower branches of my tree. I don't know if he knew I was above him, but he didn't try to climb higher. Soon—I think it was soon, anyway, for I had little sense of the passage of time and I will never know whether it was two hours or more like twenty minutes that I was up in that tree—soon the park was full and the police had driven the demonstrators to the brick wall at the other end. Somehow the fright of that irregular crew flared into rage, and picking up sticks, stones, bricks, and what little there was around them they drove the police back to the edge of the park. But the cops regrouped under their taunts, during the standoff that followed, and I saw them remove something, either their badges or their name tags, from the front of their uniforms. Now we were really in for it.

They moved back into the park with renewed brutality. They spotted the guy below me in the tree and wrestled him down. A cop gave him a mighty belt in the kidneys with his stick and he went half crawling, half limping off. At any rate, he had distracted them from me: they did not see me clinging to the smaller swaying branches above. Moments later a man was knocked unconscious under my tree. Once a cop did spot me up there, and he and some others circled around and screamed for me to come down. I didn't, though, and no one seemed to want to come up after me. As the action thinned out and the screaming grew less frequent and more remote, I saw a young woman in a white uniform kneel before the unconscious man below me. Her features were Oriental and she wore an armband with a red cross. A cop spotted her and lifted his club menacingly. She raised a thin, bare, delicate arm, ineffectually. I heard a sickening *thwock* as he struck her head and then she lay there unconscious, too, across the man she had come to help. I fought back nausea. I had caught a whiff of mace in the beginning and now again the sharp sweet-stinging smell of tear gas wafted through the park.

Finally the thing seemed expended. I got down shakily, stepping around the two unconscious bodies, and walked gingerly along the edge of the park. The police were about, but they seemed not to notice me. Although I carried the key to my mother's room in the Hilton I saw that I would not be able to cross the street. I walked down to another hotel where I knew some friends were staying.

At last someone steered me to an empty room with a bed, where I could sit and get a grip on myself. As happens so often in violent encounters, my most extreme reaction had been postponed to the aftermath.

"God, you're pale, Allen," said someone.

I felt a hand on my forehead.

"He's cold; he's clammy."

"Go lie down, Allen. Put your feet up," said a voice full of authority. "Wrap a blanket around your shoulders. Get warm."

I obeyed. Whenever I closed my eyes I saw a pattern of blue helmets, like ant eggs in a swarm or something seen through a microscope. From my high perspective, the police had been abstracted into the bobbing, weaving pale blue tops of their helmets.

They sent Norbie to the same room.

"Did you get beat up?"

"No."

"Me neither!"

Our meeting released something. We both laughed with relief, for each other, for ourselves.

Norbie explained to me how he had moved with the ebb and flow of the crowd, like a jellyfish in the surf, and had avoided any sharp clash. When he finished, I told him my story. Then he retold his story, and we remained there for a long time, telling each other what had happened over and over again in quick, low, hushed, breathless voices.

The next day he and I left Chicago and drove all night straight through to Princeton. My father, it turned out, had been watching the violence on TV at home with my two sisters. The coverage was splendid, and in a certain way he had seen more than I. A few nights later at a party, I had an argument with the wife of a professor. She argued that the demonstrators were just as much responsible for the violence as the police. It was my first of several such clashes.

I was sitting in Flo's window, on the wide sill, my legs drawn up. I was watching the lengthening afternoon shadow of the house engulf her mother's garden. Flo's portable record player, the one she would take back to college in a week or so, was set up on her dresser. It was the Beatles.

Flo was lying on her stomach on her bed. She had a book open before her and she chewed thoughtfully on a pencil.

"Allen, do you think it's all right?"

We had both vacillated on the question of sex. At times she had been vehemently in favor of it, and I had been opposed, and at other times the reverse had been true. Earlier, in the spring, I had told her that I was seriously thinking of renouncing sex altogether because of my interest in the practice of yoga. She had little sympathy for my interest in yoga; she had no understanding of the magnetic power which religion was beginning to assert in my life. Now, at the end of

August, the idea of renouncing sex, which had become the emblem of our intimacy, was unthinkable for me.

"Yeah, Flo, I think it's all right as long as we're both honest and we're not wounding each other."

"We may love each other, but we've made no formal commitment to each other. And it seems to me that we're taking something from each other that we have no right to give."

When she spoke like this I heard the voice of convention—the suffocating letter of the law. And even as she argued with me she wanted to be convinced that we had the right to love each other as deeply as we could.

Several days later my mother called upstairs to me early in the morning telling me that there was a phone call.

"Hello."

"Allen, I've got to see you right away."

"Where should we meet, Flo?"

"The garden at the graduate school . . ."

Twenty-five minutes later my emotional world crashed down at my feet. She told me that her mother had found the birth-control pills, and had accused her of being a "fornicator" and a sinner. And she told me then and there that we could no longer have sex. The humiliation of her mother's indictment of her had broken something in her. Suddenly I became the guilty party and the destroyer, who had summoned her into an illicit relationship. She said over and over to me, "Why are you trying to destroy me?"

"My feelings for you are not based on sex. Whether we have sex or not I'll continue to love you."

She walked back down the middle of Benson Road, framed by the cathedral arch of the sycamore trees. We had been cast out of Eden.

I continued to see Flo during the last weeks of the summer, and our meetings were characterized by a tender restraint. Several days after our meeting in the graduate-school garden, I met her mother in the kitchen of their house. She began to receive me with her usual warmth and friendliness, but suddenly stopped, drew herself up, and turned toward me with the cold, inquisitorial eye of a parent facing the seducer of her child.

"Allen, how could you do this?" she said.

"I love Flo," I answered.

"The Bible tells us that fornication is wrong."

Something inside me knew that what she said was right. Flo's mother considered herself a good practicing Catholic. If like many intellectual American Catholics she would consider the church's position on birth control in need of liberalizing, birth control in conjunction with premarital sex *for her own daughter* was a quantum leap that left her in a frenzy of righteous indignation. What guilt she heaped on poor Flo, who was told that she had violated her parents' trust. I wondered what Mrs. Battle was doing rummaging around in her daughter's top drawer if she trusted her so much, but that point was obscured in the ensuing bedlam. I was also angry at Flo, who had chosen to teeter so precariously on the edge of her own ambivalence. It was a temptation, but surely one that should have been fought, to let fate tip the scales when the balance of her opposing tendencies turned out to be so nearly equal. Flo, as far as I was concerned, had shirked the responsibilities of adulthood.

I remember the evening as lots of giggling and music, and fragments of lyrics: ". . . TV dinners by the pool, gee, I'm glad I finished school . . . she's only thirteen and she knows how to nasty . . . vegetables are your friends . . ." Here I was sitting in Harry Stern's room the night before registration and stoned—no, that was too weak a word—*bouldered* on LSD. Harry was a nice guy from Oklahoma who had a pet rat named Uno and Harry was obviously going to be our drug connection. All I had to do was trundle down from my new single room on the third floor of good old Cannon Hall —proof that everything was going downhill in the world was that the old dorms were the best in any school—and wonderful Harry would sell me whatever I needed at a reasonable, affordable price. This tab of LSD was a free sample from a new batch that had come from Knoxville in a slim briefcase. Uno was having some, too.

We tripped all night and by eight A.M. I was still stoned. I went to registration and obtained a little packet of computer cards full of little square holes. There were all these long lines of people and none of it made any sense to me and besides, I couldn't seem to get past the packet of cards. I stared at them for a long, long time. I opened them up and riffled them. I dived in and went for a swim. And when I came up I had to bag the whole thing and go for a walk.

I wandered into the chapel, All Saints Chapel, which was a reproduction of a chapel at Oxford. There they were, all those $25,000 stained-glass windows, and the sun was shining through and throwing a veritable symphony of color, all of them jingling and jangling against each other on the polished floor. The sun was moving ever so slowly and changing the pattern little by little. Seeing all this took hours.

When I was finished there was still time to go to the dean's office and change my major from English to history. It was a whim under a powerful drug and probably had come because I had done well in the couple of history courses I had taken. I was able to concentrate and relate to things a little better by this time, and I was even coherent during my short interview with the dean. By the time I went back to registration the lines were shorter and my concentration was still better and somehow I got the thing accomplished. Even when the drug wore off I decided that whether I was a history major or an English major made little difference.

On returning to Sewanee I had found that my disaffection with the status quo had reached the breaking point. I felt that I had no inner resources, and the external world was so hateful that I could barely stand contact with it. I discovered soon after I returned to Sewanee that many students felt that the cops had been right in Chicago. After my summer of campaigning I no longer cherished any illusions about representative government or the democratic process. It was a mug's game in which power was the coin of the realm. I didn't go to classes; I was taking a lot of drugs, smoking marijuana every day. I simply couldn't stand the way I felt. I wanted a change, but knew no way of changing myself. Caught in this impasse, I bailed out in favor of oblivion.

On surfacing from my forays into the abyss, I would go down to visit John Bessin at his house on the edge of the campus. His stability and compassionate nature had a calming effect on me.

It was one October evening when I was sipping wine at the Bessins' that Flo tracked me down by phone. During the first weeks of my drug torpor, the thought of her visiting in early October was the only light that flickered in my imagination. I went into John's study, closed the door and picked up the phone.

"Hello."

"Allen."

"Yes, Flo, how *are* you?"

"I'm okay."

"What flight are you getting into Chattanooga Airport?"

"That's just what I called to tell you about. I'm not coming to Sewanee to visit you."

"Why not?"

"I've started seeing a psychiatrist and I think it's better that we not see each other. Our relationship has been really confusing for me and I think I need time to be alone and straighten out my thinking on a lot of issues. I don't think that our being together has been constructive for either one of us. I know you've put a lot of energy into me, on which you've gotten no return. I think you may be a great person and I want you to be free to use all your powers to find out who you are and to become the person you should be."

I knew that what she was saying was as painful for her as it was for me, yet she spoke with such clarity and conviction.

I felt she was right, and that she was saving us. The truth of her words did not fill the emptiness I felt at the prospect of her not visiting me.

"I'll worry about my energy. What about yours?"

"Me? I've been losing my mind. But now I'm better. I'm going to a shrink and he says I'm a compulsive neurotic."

"Flo? Is there some kind of conflict between me and your mental health? How can that be?"

"I don't know, Allen, this is just the way I see it."

I was conscious that her voice, strained and unnaturally high, was coming to me over hundreds of miles of wire. What powers of persuasion could I manifest over that distance? I saw nothing to do but accept her verdict.

When I rejoined the group in the living room I told John what had happened. He and Margaret listened with concern, yet I could tell that John's concern for me was not the pity one feels for a wounded animal, but an interest in a young man's struggles with life and love. He said to me: "If you're going to love, you're going to suffer, Allen. There's no escaping it; it's your birthright."

The first month or six weeks of college that year was the worst of what I later termed the period of my abyss. There was a curious timelessness about this long motiveless wallow in apathy and drugs. And then, abruptly, it ended one evening in late October, just as a season will sometimes seem to end or begin in a single day, when, for instance, a cold wind arrives and we know summer is over and fall has arrived.

Ironically, the decision to clean up and give up drugs was made under the influence of drugs. I suppose Preston Ogilvey served as the catalyst for my quick change. I had taken a quarter tab of LSD and spent the early evening with Preston, who had put his sail up to catch quite a different wind that was blowing across America. This was the era when the Beatles were getting into transcendental meditation and studying under their guru, and Preston was interested in cabalistic, magical things. He read Crowley, the magician of the twenties and thirties who was back in print and enjoying a big come-back. Preston dabbled as well in astral projection, which was the flashiest mysticism going, and claimed some success at this art of sending the soul wandering apart from the body. All this he did while being a serious student in psychology and taking baths and being tidy.

"You were born for better things than burning out your brain with drugs," Preston told me.

I studied him with drug-heightened interest. He had bright blue eyes and fierce red hair. He wore an enormous handlebar moustache that practically joined his muttonchop sideburns. Such whiskers soon became commonplace, but to me then he seemed as exotic as a Charles Dickens character come to life.

We went to see a movie and, while watching it, I decided he was right about everything we had talked about. Walking back, I vowed that from then on there was going to be no booze, drugs, cigarettes or sex in my life. It was a decision as extreme as it was impulsive, but amazingly I stuck to it, basi-cally, though there were lapses.

Although I don't think it would be fair to say it was a change merely for the sake of change, it was a change amid many winds of change. Perhaps there was little reason for student radicalism to be linked to the use of strong hallucinogenic drugs, but at this time and place for me they were. To be a student radical was to admit despair and to live on the edge of desperation. As much as men like my father carrying the White Man's Burden needed alcohol, so did a peace-marching, draft-dodging student dissenter need his pot, mescaline and LSD. Similarly, mysticism, of which I now had the smallest taste in my mouth, flowed in some other direction, away from drugs. This was all the more interesting because drugs could, as they had for me, make the mind more receptive to mysticism.

I started to move in a different set. I still saw Martin and

Galen, and for that matter things were improving for them. I'm not sure the improvement entirely pleased them, particularly Martin, the declared communist for whom there was a long tradition of worse being better. But opinion was shifting, even at Sewanee, and last year's radicals were being sucked into next year's mainstream. A key indicator was Ralph Price, the campus chaplain. Price was a strong, well-built fellow from Arkansas with ruddy skin, thick black hair and an intelligence that had been sharpened with study abroad, at Oxford. Sharpened maybe even to too fine a point, because sometimes Price gave the impression of holding something in reserve, of talking down to youth. Perhaps his intelligence conflicted with his broad avowal to uphold Sewanee's traditions, but at any rate in the fall of 1968 he crumpled to the burgeoning will of the students and came out against the war and for peace.

I also met Quincy Fay, another nonfraternity boy and dorm lizard who played the violin, practiced yoga and jogged, long before the fitness boom. We became vegetarians. We did so largely in the spirit of the Hindu belief that one's relationship with animals should be one of harmlessness. We also equated eating meat with greedy, selfish, unbalanced, winner-take-all imperialism. Gobbling chickens, gorging on steaks, one took up too much room, loomed too large and somehow, full of slaughterhouse death screams and a surplus of blood, ended up frying peaceful peasants in napalm in some far-off other world.

We discovered him not thirteen miles away—Deh Chun, a Chinese monk living on a hillside amid his simple vegetable garden of peas, carrots and sweet potatoes, on which he lived, even, apparently, through the winter. We found him charming, though he, in fact, refused to exert any leadership role at all. He was hospitable to us, in his simple way. He would pull up crates for us to sit on and serve us green tea. He seemed both puzzled and pleased by this ripple of admiration falling so unexpectedly upon his shore. What a simple, pleasant life he seemed to live. He would sit by his window and do traditional-looking ink drawings of boats passing through clouds.

In looks, wearing a little thin Oriental moustache, he was rather like a Chinese film pirate. He was slender, about five-foot-six. His clothing was our only disappointment, a small one. He did not wear saffron robes, he wore jeans and T-shirts. Deh Chun always seemed to be sitting on the floor or squatting on his haunches, Oriental style. He had unwrapped bolts of cloth to cover the windows. Looking around his hut, we could imagine that he had moved in two weeks ago. Actually, this modest Chinese man had been in Tennessee for seven years.

We read the Tao Te Ching, and imagining that we were seeing these eighty-one poems of the sage of the Chou dynasty through Deh Chun's eyes helped us. The idea of mastering one's nature through simplicity and restraint shed light on the experiences of the past year.

> He whose desires are few gets them,
> He whose desires are many, loses his way.

This was the right path. I would sit in the half-lotus position against the wall in my dorm room and repeat prayers of renunciation to myself.

I began attending my classes—just about every one of them—not out of interest, but solely for the sake of self-discipline. Classes assumed the dubious importance of fence-posts counted on the way to somewhere. Needless to say, I did not learn anything much. I also became intolerant of the usual extracurricular frivolousness and blather. During this time people who dropped into my room found me intolerant of conversation that did not have God at its center.

If I was not going to become a doctor, or a lawyer, or a broker on Wall Street, if my real desire in life was to transcend the world and become a saint, then I would do it with the singleminded devotion and furious energy of a miser hoarding and collecting his stockpile of gold. I remember a conversation with Father Ralston, an Episcopal priest at Sewanee, and a boy named Steve Zimmerman, out on the edge of the mountain overlooking the valley. I was telling Father Ralston about my interest in spirituality and yoga.

I'll never forget. He said, "Beware of purification. In place of the seven demons you cast out, you will find that you have made room for seven greater demons to come in." I refused his advice, and in refusing, opened the door to the enactment of his prophecy. Surely the wisdom of the East was accessible in many ways.

Each path in life, whether it's the philosophy of Wittgenstein or the poetry of Lao-tzu, also has its sensual aspects, its atmosphere, as palpable as the trodden clay underfoot, as elusive as a whiff of old linen paper, ink and leather bindings. To me the East was exotic and I loved its exoticism.

Perhaps my concentration was disturbed or possibly the experience of reading the yogis was so pithy, so much to be savored quite apart from the spirit in which a college student is encouraged to read two hundred pages of history a night, but at any rate my reading was reduced to a mere couple of pages of Rama Krishna each evening. Nineteenth-century India seemed to me such a place of innocence. Even in the twentieth-century India of Yogananda, God seemed immanent, gentle and smiling, apprehensible, ever so different from the God of my father, and forefathers, who was demanding, remote, and yet certain to punish.

If in some deep and scarcely conscious sense I was disgusted with myself—for not studying, for wallowing, for not achieving the goals and mastering the way of my parents and my society—very likely I sought to mortify and punish myself. That might account for my attraction to a rigid and demanding path that was spurned by everyone else. If that was the state of my unconscious processes, then nothing could have satisfied them better than the disease that I proceeded to contract, the great sapper of vitality, of the will: mononucleosis. I discovered I had mono while I was in Atlanta visiting a friend whose father was a doctor and who diagnosed the malady. I returned to Sewanee and stayed in the hospital for a week.

I found the experience fantastic. I felt like I was burning all the poisons out, like I was being purified. I had high fevers and then copious sweats. When a kindly nurse wanted to rub my body with alcohol, I refused to let her do so. I refused not so much because such sexually tinged sensualism was clearly evil as because some inner voice told me it was wrong. That was the way The Way was, subtle, paradoxical, difficult to explain except to the initiated, to whom it was clear. Also at this time, during those feverish nights, what previously had been the inkling of a temptation began to blossom into a full-fledged compulsion. I must leave, escape, hitchhike across the country. When I got to the West Coast and the Pacific Ocean, I would not stop. I would manage, saving pennies or working my passage, somehow to go to India, where I would continue to follow the ultimate enlightenment, the only path that had ever made any sense to me. The details were yet to be settled. Perhaps I would simply wander and beg, a penniless ascetic, like the Sadhana of *Siddhartha*.

So it was that, not long after I left the hospital and two days before spring vacation, I put all my possessions except for essentials—a few clothes to wear and a couple of yoga books—out in the dorm hall for the other students to pick over. By the time I left for home, my luggage was light. I had only to shed the looming burden of telling my parents of my decision and I would be free.

They did not take it as badly as I expected. My father was deeply worried about me and feared I was doing something rash that I would ever after regret. Yet what could he do? He was presented with the *fait accompli*. It was perfectly clear that if I did go back to Sewanee, nothing could repair my months of neglect and semesters of bad grades. Besides, the mono presented a plausible excuse. It was a long and lingering disease. I was psychologically down and maybe it would be better for me to hang around and take it easy.

My mother even looked for sparkles of silver on the underside. If my decision was totally unwelcome in itself, maybe the good part was that at last I had made some decision. Maybe here at last was the assertion of independence that could be built upon.

They were also consumed, particularly my mother, with the fear that their sons would be drafted and slaughtered. If I could be saved from that doom, they would have plenty of time to patch me up later. And here I was blithely making this choice, which would have as one of its main consequences the loss of my student deferment. I seemed oblivious to such worldly cares. I had not imagined, in my wildest fantasy of myself wandering in India with a begging bowl, that I would have to carry a draft card tucked in my humble loincloth.

There had just been a crisis and a close call with Pete. He had been safely headed for a Peace Corps stint, having just finished training, when he was abruptly bounced, and for no reason the Peace Corps cared to make public. I would soon find out the real reason, but for now the important thing was that Pete had finally yielded and had applied for and gotten his C.O. deferment, which everyone agreed was the only possible course. So Pete was safe.

Allen turned out to be not nearly as hard to take care of. Allen was in quite a malleable state in regard to such worldly cares as saving his own hide. My father made an appointment with a psychologist. So one weekday I picked up my sister Amy from her Catholic country day school and drove the few miles to the New Jersey Neuropsychiatric Hospital. It was a handsome institution of nineteenth-century red-brick buildings situated on a couple of hundred green acres on the way to Belle Meade. Amy was coming because she hoped she would get a free test from the psychologist who did the testing for my father's clinic.

I had been helping Amy memorize poetry and now I quizzed

her. She recited in a serious voice as we drove through the spring afternoon in the family car:

> And he was rich—yes richer than a king—
> And admirably schooled in every grace:
> In fine, we thought that he was everything
> To make us wish that we were in his place.

It was Edwin Arlington Robinson's "Richard Cory," about the envied man who had it all and "went home and put a bullet through his head." This American poet had perfectly delineated the gap in the national identity that I regarded as my starting point.

"Good, Amy, you've got it down perfectly." I glanced over at her for a moment, worried that the macabre subject matter might have disturbed her. But no, she seemed unperturbed and simply happy to be going on an adventure with her big brother. She smiled and the bright sunlight filled her blue eyes and made a shimmering halo of her pale hair in the wind.

I swerved onto the rolling grounds, which resembled a golf course, and found the trailer-like affair on a green mowed island in the middle of this institution, the so-called state snake pit where the people who were not getting well came to live. For all of that, there was not a bar visible on the large windows. It was quiet and peaceful under the large maples and oaks, like a campus.

Mustapha Gahli was the head psychologist in charge of tests. He was a short, neat man in shirtsleeves—his jacket hung behind him—and glasses. He had olive skin and he was Egyptian.

Dr. Gahli gave me the Minnesota Multiphasic Personality Test which consisted of hundreds of yes or no questions, for instance: Are dogs smiling at you? (No.) And will Christ return before the year 2000? (I said yes.) Dr. Gahli inspired trust, radiated competence, and his questions, when he interviewed me, were not patronizing. Some of the questions were way out, and some were ideologically loaded, or so I thought. We ended up talking about philosophy and poetry, about yoga and about mystic experiences. I told him about an out-of-body experience I had had as a child. I also told him about a vision of a big green stone, a mandala, that Hindu and Buddhist symbol of the universe, a square within a circle, which had seemed to hover over me as I closed my eyes just before sleep, also when I was a child. I told him that lately I had been seeing the hovering green stone mandala again. This interested him.

"You know," said Dr. Gahli warmly, standing there limpid-eyed in the afternoon light, "when I was a bright young student I had a choice of two scholarships, one to go to England and study psychiatry and another to go to India and study mysticism. Now I sometimes wonder if I made the right choice."

The personality test was scored along a bell curve. My responses to reality were found to be several standard deviations off the mean. It was explained to me that this did not mean that I was crazy. It simply meant that I was probably in a state that was very different from everybody else's. Dr. Gahli also must have decided that this state was a fragile one, because he testified that he thought I would crack in combat. My draft board classified me 1-Y, deferred until a national emergency.

Two lapses in the month of April reminded me that there had been great wisdom in my vow to Preston Ogilvie back in October not to smoke—neither cigarettes nor dope—and not to screw, drink or use other drugs. It contained the wisdom of Epicurus: cultivate your garden. It had protected me from stress that I was scarcely in any state to bear.

I went down to Philadelphia to visit Norbie at Penn. In the spirit of keeping up with an old pal, I decided it would be fun to take mescaline. I knew I shouldn't, but Norbie was going to, and I did. We went out to an Italian restaurant—he, I and his date—and by the time the eggplant parmesan arrived the onion of Allen had shed all of its skins and I was left without an identity. I looked at the food. I did not know how to eat it. I was a beached jellyfish. I couldn't move. Norbie, who had taken the same dose but fortunately had an ironclad psyche, perceived my trouble. They took me outside and guided me to a chicken-wire fence. I hooked my fingers through it and clung, looking at life through a net. Then Norbie talked to me the way one does to people in such states.

"Allen, are you okay?" asked Norbie.

I replied hesitantly, "Wow, man, I think I'm really losing it."

"Do you want to go home?"

"I don't think I can handle this restaurant anymore. Do you think you could get me back to your apartment?" I said in a shaky voice.

They were able to get me back to Norbie's, where he called up his younger brother Bruce and asked him to come over and stay with me. I talked to Bruce on the phone and had a total precognition of the whole conversation. When he came over, we smoked dope and talked, and everything was okay until the others got back. But when I woke up the next morning, I couldn't seem to talk. Furthermore, I had nothing to say.

Flo precipitated the next lapse. I went up to visit her in Boston. She smuggled me into her room, where I slept on the floor, wrapped in her extra blankets on a pile of coats.

"I don't mind sleeping on the floor," I told her just before we turned out the lights. "Do you remember how you used to ask me what was I going to do with my life? Well, now I know. I'm going to become a *sannyasin*, a total renunciate. I'm going to hitch across the country and work my passage to India. I'm not going to have any social position. No name, even. For all intents and purposes, according to the way we used to talk, I have no future. I'm free of all that now. And soon I'll be sleeping in lots of strange uncomfortable places."

The next day we went looking for a mutual friend on another

campus. We never did find him. We spent the day lying on the new grass—it was late April by now—and talking incessantly.

Flo didn't like the idea of my becoming a *sannyasin*. I think she probably saw it as an attempt to escape from reality, a refusal to grow up. There was no way for me to make myself clear to her. Her thinking at this point was largely informed by her weekly meetings with a Freudian analyst, and I think she saw that security for her lay in trying to embrace conventional goals.

We ended up waiting for Eddie Grant that evening in his dorm suite, which he shared with two other guys. Flo and I went to sleep in his bed, together, in one another's arms, while across the bedroom his two suitemates slept in their beds. After they were asleep, or seemed to be asleep, Flo told me that she wanted to make love in these strange circumstances.

I cherished Flo. I wanted to be warm and kind. I wanted this to bring us closer. But I had little or no physical desire for her at this time. Reluctantly, I obliged her and we fell asleep.

The next morning she was consumed with guilt. We rushed back to her dorm at the university, missing our friend altogether. On the bus, her dark hair rumpled and the sleep creases still on her face, she told me: "This is wrong, Allen. I can't say why, but I'm filled with dread—with fear, Allen, and I don't know of what or why."

Her hand tightened around my wrist.

"Oh, why did we do it? It was so wrong."

"You wanted to," I reminded her. The fear was infectious. I knew it would drive me from her. I could say nothing to comfort her. As soon as we arrived at her room, I would pack my stuff and leave.

I hardly realized it at the time, but in making these visits I was bidding my farewells. Next came my brother Pete down in Washington. Pete was newly married to a young woman he had met in Peace Corps training. In fact, she was the reason they were busted out. Shortly after they were married, she had told officials in Putney, Vermont, where they were training to go to Brazil, that she had smoked marijuana. That was an absolute no-no; the Peace Corps did not want any pot-smoking characters.

I took an instant dislike to my brother's new wife, Kathleen, which was disturbing, to say the least. As far as I was concerned the evidence was plain that she had foiled their chance to serve in Brazil.

I found my brother living in a small apartment on the fringes of Georgetown near the P-Street Bridge. Pete was going to Georgetown grad school in Latin American studies during the day and working nights in a warehouse. There seemed to be nothing for me to say to Pete. Furthermore, there seemed to be little time in which to say it. His schedule was killing.

I hung around a few days. Since Pete was either working, attending classes, studying or sleeping and since I didn't want to stay and talk to Kathleen, I found myself drawn to Dupont Circle, just over the P-Street Bridge, which spanned no waterway, but rather the great ravine of Rock Creek Park, where Teddy Roosevelt used to take his vigorous daily constitutionals. It was the hippie scene, a kind of California park scene in the middle of the city. There I made my first black friend, Leroy, who worked in the post office. We drank beer together and went to whatever parties we heard about in the circle.

My farewell to Pete was my last one, a sad one. I felt he was locked into a sad marriage and a life of overwork. My parents were vacationing in Portugal and there was little reason for me to return to Princeton.

There was nothing to do but take a deep breath and do what I had been dreaming of and talking about for so long. Act! A quick glance at the map showed that the closest of the main arteries west fed out of Harrisburg, Pennsylvania. I took a bus to Harrisburg. I arrived in the early afternoon. I asked about the fares to San Francisco and decided I would do better to hitch, since I had only about $150 in my pocket. I went to the station cafeteria and had a solemn meal of overcooked meatloaf and limp string beans that were beginning to acquire the texture of wet cardboard. I got a cab and rode out to Route 76 west, the Pennsylvania Turnpike.

It was about four-thirty and there I was, wearing a strange pair of pointed sharkskin shoes, once expensive, now beat up, a blue shirt and baggy olive-green pants. As I waited, I lit up a cigarette. My vow of seven months ago was shattered, of course, and I now smoked, both dope and tobacco, drank, used drugs and screwed. Was I on the run or going somewhere? I got two short rides and then ended up at a Howard Johnson's somewhere about eight o'clock.

I didn't know where I was, but one thing about Howard Johnson America is that it is everywhere and nowhere. Hojo's was invented and prospered precisely because a Hojo is always the same. So America could travel without traveling. I went in and had a quality-controlled cup of coffee, surprisingly good, and then dropped my baggage near the parking lot, where I hoped to pick up a ride from someone coming out.

Here came this guy with a battered suitcase and a guitar and he smiled. I thought I had a ride, but the smile was for camaraderie, because he was hitchhiking, too. He was going to Oakland, and naturally we decided to carry on together. A trucker gave us a ride, and the truckers turned out to be the kindest ole boys on the road. They often stopped during that long night, they were always nice, and early in the morning one picked us up and let us sleep in the double bunk up in back of the cab. It was heaven for us. By morning we were outside Chicago; and my companion invited me to come with him to a friend's in Gary, Indiana. The friend was a grade-school art teacher who would let us sleep on his floor. I welcomed the chance for a break. I was only a third of the way to the Coast, but I was exhausted. Hitching was a tense, anxious business.

That night we went into Chicago, which I still found, for all my violent memories, a beautiful lakeside city. We went to a hippie coffeehouse, where everybody was stoned on something and dancing to strobes. There was this black guy, this spade dude, as he would be called in the lingo of the alienated youth (which was at least bringing the races closer together). He told us he had just returned from Jupiter. He was far gone on LSD, but after assuring us that there was much to be learned on Jupiter, he helped us to score some acid. We took it back to the house, ground it up and sniffed it.

It worked right away; we were rocketing off. It turned out to be an evening of monologues. I waxed lyrically eloquent on God, yoga and spiritualism, and I felt, for the time, in full possession of the truth. I imparted it in the form of my life story.

Then it was my companion's turn. He was a skinny, scruffy, pale fellow in his mid-twenties, hook-nosed and hatchet-faced. He rather resembled Bob Dylan and when he sang antiwar ballads, accompanying himself on his guitar, I don't suppose he was too much worse at carrying a tune. He was an ex-Marine, had been at the siege of Khe Sanh, where he had seen a Vietnamese girl of about fourteen gang-raped and then thrown out into the free-fire zone to be ripped apart in the crossfire. He had gone psycho at Khe Sanh, but he had survived and been taken out to a hospital, where for nine months he still thought he was at Khe Sanh. He had come out of it not so long ago, and now he was on his way to Oakland to find his girl and to become a songwriter.

I imagined him to be a typical working-class kid who joined the Marines to see the world. What worlds he had seen now. He had pale blue, almost blind-looking eyes, and now they were the seared eyes of a soldier. I imagined he could watch a beheading or a wedding with the same detachment. He seemed at once gentle and full of violence. I regarded him, after I had heard his story, as the burned-out shell of a man, with a voice. So now he was the troubadour, bard and prophet who had seen to the very heart of things.

Early that morning, when we finally went to sleep, I dreamed that America, the whole country behind me, all that I was leaving, was burning. It was a wide, low fire, like a prairie fire, and it moved across the country in a line, fast, and I was running ahead of it. This was to become a recurring dream during the next few weeks. As to the question I had asked when I had begun hitchhiking, I now had my answer. It didn't take a psychoanalyst to tell me I was running away from something.

In the morning we went over to a church soup kitchen run by some radical-chic Presbyterian clergy. You could eat for free, but the catch was that you had to listen to what was going on. Everything was going on. Everyone was there. The Young Lords were, preaching militant black radicalism, full of anger and energy, talking about how they were just about fed up and just on the verge of really getting out in the streets and murdering the pigs. The Progressive Labor Party was there, now fragmented over the issue of Marxist purity into PLP-I and PLP-II and at each other's throats, but in general explaining every little thing in terms of their doctrinaire Marxism. What a group of passionate paranoiacs they were. In common with the Young Lords, they could speak of chilling random violence with utter righteousness. The evangelical Christians were asking were we washed in the blood of the lamb, and blissed-out Hare Krishnas, wearing robes and with their hair shaved to topknots, were chanting. This soup kitchen was like a storybook jungle watering hole where beasts of every stripe and claw came down to mingle. And all these souls were equally lost, I thought. I was not particularly disturbed. Perhaps it was the leftover of the acid, but I wondered at what a beautiful and strange place Chi-

66 :

cago was. Once again it was here in this great stockyard
and slaughterhouse of a city that the underbelly of life was
revealed to me.

On the third day the vet and I left Chicago by way of
a ride along old Route 66, which ran through Missouri and
Oklahoma. Someplace out on the prairie we got a ride with
an odd blond fellow on his way to a new job in Oakland.
Fine. We traveled with him all the way. He had a spank-
ing new sporty Detroit car and a funny cast to one eye which
turned out to be glass. So we barreled along at 115 miles an
hour through New Mexico and Arizona, where the highway
patrol stopped us and searched the car, but fortunately we
didn't have so much as a dustspeck of dope left.

This was my first cross-country drive; I had never really
seen the West. I enjoyed the weird lunar landscape of New
Mexico. The climate was exotically extreme. In the morning,
when we went into a restaurant, it was about fifty degrees
outside, pleasant. By the time we came out it was scorching,
and the inside of the car, when we clambered back in, was
like an oven.

We didn't stop often, though. We made the trip from
Chicago to Laguna Beach in thirty or thirty-two hours. When
I dozed in the back seat I again dreamed that this country
we were moving across was burning behind us, the houses,
trees and buildings all going up in crackling orange flames
and billowing black smoke. Sometimes as I stared out the
window in a traveling stupor I thought I could just about see
the fire over the horizon.

We arrived at the one-eyed man's destination in the early
morning. My companion and I got out silently and started
walking. I was carrying a suitcase and a duffel bag, while
the vet was loaded more lightly. He got farther and farther
ahead of me, as I occasionally stopped to shift my grip or
rest briefly. Finally, he disappeared. I looked for him in the
growing early morning light and he was simply not there.

I stopped and a shiver went down my back. For a moment I had the eerie feeling that he had not been real, that perhaps he had really been killed at Khe Sanh and that he now had served, the spectre of a wasted generation, as my guide along this cross-country road, more barren than I could ever have imagined.

I got myself oriented and picked up a short ride to San Diego. I dumped my gear in a bus-station locker and walked around. This was California and the Pacific Ocean was in sight. Was I at my destination? I didn't know. I was ready to put up my sail in any reasonable wind, and maybe this was the place. But San Diego, as I saw it, was a military town. The Navy was everywhere. The destroyers and big carriers were in the harbor and overhead many kinds of fighter planes streaked in and out of a military airport along the beach. Now and then a great rolling boom came in as one of them broke the sound barrier out over the ocean. A bar where I stopped for a beer was full of Marines who, with their lumpy-looking shaved heads, seemed incredibly young and vulnerable. They looked like boys of twelve, swilling beer, wearing immaculate uniforms with shiny shooting medals, playing pool and talking about what it was going to be like in Nam.

I took the bus up to Los Angeles. I managed to sleep a few hours on the bus, and when I arrived, I again put my gear in a locker and walked around. It was night and out on Sunset Boulevard it was the freak parade. It was a great milling, wandering-up-and-down scene, as if every displaced youth in the nation, myself included, had been by a lemming-like compulsion driven here. Mostly it was a purely social scene, too, because except for that, there was no reason for us to be here, except, of course, for the peddlers of sex, the flashy blond whores, pretty young ones in micro-minis and a look of sweet sixteen already gone sour, and their pimps, heavy-mannered loitering dudes. And the peddlers of drugs, who caught your eye and called out their wares in soft hissing voices: ups, downs and all arounds. I, however, had something to do. I needed a place to stay. I was tired, dangerously exhausted. As well as sleeping, I also needed to do something besides cope with where my next meal, ride or rest was coming from. I needed to curl up and clear my mind.

So I began asking everyone if they knew where I could find a place to stay. Contact was as easy as a smile. I got lots of easy-riding California glad-handing, but after we all did our own thing it was obvious nobody was going to do anything for me. Here we were in this May, two years after the Summer of Love, 1967, and generosity was worn paper thin, was a mere costume under which all these frayed, booted, long-haired, denim-clad freaks couldn't have seemed meaner to me than a Wall Street crowd of straights wearing pinstripes and cordovan clodhoppers. The only offers I got were from several homosexuals, a particularly rapacious-looking and sinister-seeming kind that preyed on the drug-fuddled youth scene. At about four A.M. I checked into a five-dollar fleabag hotel.

The next day I bused up to San Francisco and on to Berkeley, which I had heard was a wide-open, freewheeling place with what L.A. so sadly lacked, a sense of community. Things did begin to get much better at Berkeley, because right away I found my way to a Catholic church that offered baths to the drifting public, and I was immensely refreshed with a shower and a shave, which I had not gotten at the fleabag flophouse. I went on to the park-like campus, with its modern buildings and walkway arteries pulsing with youth at the change of classes. It was a sunny, mild day, and a cool breeze rattled through the palm trees as I made my way to the student union.

A wonderful bulletin board was there. It was a community in itself, and people were constantly browsing there. It offered everything: goods, services, deals, riches, car pools, cars, and places to live, even places where I could stay for a month start on my tiny bankroll. I copied down some addresses and phone numbers. I wondered what I could do with my stuff while I looked. I decided I would write a note of my own, asking if anyone knew where I could leave my baggage. Yet how would they contact me? I had no place, no phone. Well, I decided I would sign my note, "Allen, at the foot of the steps," and I would wait there with my gear and hope someone would offer me help. This might well be a good way to find a floor or a couch to sleep on this very evening. I got a piece of paper out of my bag. But I had no pen. I asked to borrow one from a bearded student sitting next to me. He watched over my shoulder as I wrote with his yellow ballpoint.

"I know a place," he said when I had finished. "It's a sort of religious community. It's called the Unified Family. Come, I'll show you."

He took my duffel bag and I carried my suitcase as he guided me down Telegraph Avenue. On the way we had one of those conversations that were so typical of the era:

"What sign are you?" he asked.

"Aries."

"Far out! I am, too. What year were you born?"

"Forty-seven."

"Wow! Me, too. We're exactly the same age. What decan are you in?"

"First."

"That's just too much. Me, too. Man, we're really on the same wavelength."

My guide had long hair and a beard and by the time we had turned into the walk of a nondescript yellow clapboard house he had told me he was an ex-heroin addict from the Haight who had cleaned up and now lived in this "sort of commune."

"Thank you," I said as he put my duffel bag in a first-floor closet. "It was a lucky conincidence you were there."

"Oh, it wasn't a coincidence. It was prophetic," he said, smiling.

I raised my eyebrows in mild puzzlement, but he held my gaze, kept his smile and didn't explain.

"Can you wait here a minute? There's someone I want you to meet."

Padding down the stairs came a man in his early forties who was quiet and modest and Oriental. No doubt of it, by now I had acquired a completely positive prejudice toward Orientals, both from my rejection of my own culture and my attraction to Eastern religion. Henry Muso seemed to me the picture of an Oriental sage. We sat on cushions in the living room and he asked me what I was doing. In my state, that was difficult to say, but he seemed to understand precisely. I rambled on about fleeing a materialistic society.

"Could we say that in some fashion you are seeking God?"

I replied calmly that I was searching for God. He asked me how I was doing this. I told him that I had left school, and that I was on my way to India. He responded, "We also are searching for God."

Henry Muso, I was to learn, was an Indonesian, forty-three years old, who was studying for a Ph.D. in economics at the university. He headed this commune of about a dozen people and had been in the Unified Family for six years. He had been married only a few months to his wife, Anne, who was in her early thirties. She came from Pennsylvania and had previously been a member of the Church of the Brethren.

I was invited to return for dinner and to stay for a lecture on philosophy afterwards. It was also clear that I could sleep on the floor here. Indeed, everyone in this commune lived a life of some sacrifice and self-denial, and everyone slept on the floor. I liked that.

The dinner was delicious and filling, and in my state I was very grateful for it. The lecture, by Muso, was theological. It was given in a large first-floor room, what I suppose had been the living room, only now it was more like a class-room with a blackboard at one end. The lecture was entitled "The Principle of Creation," and it was all about God, his dual characteristics, his omnipresence, give-and-take, male-and-female, prime energy, joy, good, beauty, will, emotion, the purpose of creation, growth (visible and invisible), and was all and all as easy to take as a sugar-coated pill. If it was all rather vague, it was also rather poetic, and I slept that night with a glowing sense of fullness that certainly included my belly.

I came the next night for another meal and another lecture. In this lecture, Muso endeavored to prove that the original sin which brought about the fall of man was sex, adultery, fornication. Muso often quoted the Bible in his exposition, and he favored a symbolic rather than a fundamentalist inter-pretation. Eve, for instance, was the tree of knowledge. The tree was a symbol for her. Man did not fall by eating the fruit of the tree of knowledge, for if Adam and Eve had done that they would have covered their hands and mouths for shame, Muso reasoned, not their genitals, as Genesis said they did. Eve had intercourse with the archangel Lucifer, who was jealous of the place man held in the divine creation, and she later seduced Adam. Because Adam and Eve had intercourse prematurely, before they were intended to in the divine plan, we all lived in a fallen state.

"There are other ways to prove that the root sin was adul-tery, not pride or envy," said Muso. I sat on the floor before him, cross-legged, with four or five other young people who had also been invited to the dinner and lecture. "Actually every religion which has sought to eliminate sin has stressed the ascetic life as the path to salvation and purification," Muso went on in his gentle, patient way. "The Israelites sought to purify themselves before God by circumcising themselves. That also proves that adultry and sex are the root of sin."

That night as I went to sleep on the floor in a room with four or five other guys in a borrowed sleeping bag with teddy bears on it—a child's evidently, but roomy enough for an adult—I thought about Flo. Her strange, displaced and yet intense guilt after we had had intercourse certainly jibed with what Muso had said. Of course. What she had been feeling was a deep sense of sin. It had been more intense for her than for me because, as Muso had said, Eve was far more culpable than Adam in the original sin. Yes, I thought as I drifted into the deep sleep of the exhausted, the lecture had made perfect sense.

Berkeley was a spiritual supermarket. Here was a main outpost, if not the very fortress, of youth alienated from the Great Society, as Lyndon Johnson had named it, thus putting the capstone on a structure that immediately began to crumble. These youth were the spawn of the postwar generation— scarcely one had been born before 1945—who had grown up in the sweet domestic materialism of the great suburban sprawl, amid the hum, whirr and putt of mixers, washing machines, blenders, grinders and mowers, and who began to hunger for the very things that life excluded. They had been through no Great Depression and no World War, and so it would not be enough for them to go to church on Sunday morning and thank God for a steady job and enough money to buy a voluptuous Buick and pay up the insurance premiums. They had stronger spiritual hungers, and here they were offered enough religions to satisfy any late Roman.

So I went with a guy named Norman Mayer whom I had met at my first dinner at the Unified Family, to hear Stephen speak at the Fillmore. Stephen was a Christian Karma yogi; he preached hard work, honesty, and the surrendering of the fruits of one's labor to God. Stephen later took a large group of people to Tennessee, where they founded a very successful farming community.

Mayer and I went to hear Stephen largely out of curiosity. Neither of us was much attracted. With my readings in yoga and my level of general education, incomplete as it was, I felt

far above nearly all of these California easy riders. And
Mayer had demons of his own. He was coming down from a
heavy drug experience which had driven him nearly psycho.
He still claimed to see spirits, among them a dwarf who made
himself invisible to all others and was following him around.
You could look into Mayer's big blue eyes—bluer by contrast
with the raw-red pulp of his face, for he was a blond and per-
petually sunburned by the California sun—and believe him.
Most of all because he tried to ignore the dwarf, and failed.
His eyes would be irresistibly drawn to the corner around
which the dwarf was peeping or to the chair where the dwarf
was sitting in the periphery of Mayer's vision.

Mayer was also attracted to Meher Baba, a Moslem guru
who had taken a vow of silence some forty years before. At
the end of the period of silence he was to come forward and
speak the truth to his patient followers. But, alas, Meher Baba
would die that year, in silence, before the forty years were up,
without speaking the truth. Mayer had exotic tastes. For all
that, he must have been reaching for the unattainable. I would
hear two years later that he had killed himself with an over-
dose of sleeping pills.

One afternoon I visited the Hare Krishnas. I danced in
front of a big picture of Krishna with girls wearing saris and
boys in dhotis and chanted with them: *hare krishna, hare
krishna, krishna, krishna, hare hare, hare rama, hare rama*.
We ate lots of fruit, bananas and strawberries, out of a big
plastic tub and drank the juice as well. I approved of these
people, and I knew that they were devotional yogis, *bhakti*
yogis, and followed one of the four main paths. Nevertheless,
they were not for me.

Nor was the Maharishi Mahesh Yogi, the transcendental
meditator, who had many, many adherents in California,
many of them show biz people down in Hollywood. Nor was
I pleased by the young man who ran up to me one day as I
walked down Telegraph Avenue and put his hands on my
head. "I am praying that you have your eyes opened, brother,"

he shrieked. "I am praying in the hope that you are saved from demonic possession, brother." I disengaged myself as gently as I could and walked on. Clearly, the demons he wished to deliver me from were his own.

During this week I asked almost everyone I talked to for any length of time if they knew any place where I could sleep. It was a repeat of the Sunset Boulevard experience. All doors were closed to me except the Unified Family's.

So each night—except for one when I slept out on a park bench—I returned to the Unified Family. I also ate there. The women cooked, and the food was good—simple and plentiful. There was lots of fare like meat loaf and fresh vegetables, and, when someone took the trouble, Korean, Chinese or Japanese food, which was held in high esteem. It was then that I first tasted *kimchi*, Korean pickled cabbage, which I came to love. Although about half the group on Milvia Avenue were women, there was an absolutely puritanical prohibition of any physical contact between the sexes. I well understood this chastity after hearing Henry Muso's second lecture.

Each night after dinner I went into the room with a blackboard accompanied by the two or three or four or five others who had been invited from the outside, and heard a series of lectures, each now delivered by a different member of the commune. This cycle completed a brief introduction to the teachings of a mystic born in Korea. He was mentioned by name only once.

These teachings followed the Holy Bible, although the interpretations drawn from the parables were somewhat different—but not contradictory—to what I had heard before. The philosophy underlying the teachings was dualistic, and made much of the story of Cain, who was regarded as the illicit fruit of Eve's coupling with the fallen angel, and Abel, the fruit of her second illicit coupling with Adam. The teachings had an historical aspect as well, perhaps somewhat Hegelian. The First World War was seen as a conflict of Cain nations, Moslem Turkey supported by Germany and Austria-Hungary, and the Abel nations, the Christian nations of England, America and France.

This duality continued to present times, when communism represented the Cain strain of mankind, allied with Satan, and the Western democracies represented the Abel strain, fallen, but closer to God. History worked toward restoration, and when Cain and Abel were sufficiently reconciled, the Lord of the Second Advent, the messiah, would be acclaimed. There was reason to believe, the last lecturer said, that this messiah had been born in Korea. But that belief was not a part of the body of these teachings, he said. As to who the messiah was, or when he came, at this point that was a matter of individual faith.

"Now you must decide for yourself, Allen. You must fast. You must wait until you know whether our path is yours. That time will come. There is no reason to rush yourself."

That was what Kirby Smith, the member of the commune with whom I felt most at home, said. Kirby was a Princeton graduate who had dropped out of law school. He was clearly of my own class. Kirby was certainly not a laid-back California guru. He combined an aura of spiritual leadership with the brisk upright efficiency of a college sportsman—a hockey player, perhaps.

I did fast. And on the third day, as I was bicycling across the campus, I saw a young mother and her baby under a loquat tree. The mother was trying to reach the lower branches, but they were too high. I stopped. Standing on the bike while she held it steady, I reached for the yellow fruit. I got one for her, one for the baby, and one for me. I ate part of mine before I remembered my fast. I had broken it. Then came a great dawning and a great surge of emotion. The emotion was overwhelming. If I was in a heightened emotional state just from the strain of having run away from all I knew, the fasting had multiplied it to yet another power.

I saw myself standing under the tree of knowledge, eating the forbidden fruit, having been tempted to it by a woman. Somehow, I was reenacting the fall. And somehow this proved that the teachings of the Reverend Sun Myung Moon were absolutely right.

A burden lifted from me as I pedaled hurriedly back to the house on Milvia Street. Now I had a place to sleep and eat. Friends. I had a belief and there was work to do.

So I was welcomed into the bosom of a new family. They were overjoyed. There is no religious affirmation like the conversion of an outsider. Within a week I was "witnessing," as we called the process of going out and buttonholing prospective converts. I also began giving one of the after-dinner lectures on the *Divine Principle*, as the body of the Reverend Moon's teachings was called. I took over Muso's first lecture on the principle of creation. The seeker had quickly turned into a teacher. It was not so odd. Nothing quite dispels a sense of confusion as quickly as convincing others of what to believe or do.

I remember this as an absolutely blissful time. At last the great stress and anxiety of my college existence, which had gradually and steadily gotten worse until it culminated in my cross-country flight, was relieved. This was heaven compared to that. I remember this as a time of good food, good weather, and Pollyanna love. I picked up a minimum-wage job at a fish-and-chips place run by a crazy lady. From seven until midnight I fried burgers, chicken, fish and potatoes, slopped slaw and threw together pastrami and swiss-on-rye sandwiches and was perfectly happy doing it. I was relieved of the burden of worrying about getting ahead. In this new world I had entered there was no getting ahead in that sense.

I got along well with the others, although except for Kirby, they were not really my type. Most of the group were young —at twenty-two I was the fourth oldest, after the Musos and Kirby—and about half of them were students. The rest had pickup jobs like me. Half were female, too, but it was Polly-anna love between the sexes except for one little temptation, which came in the form of Kate Dippel, a sleek blue-eyed blonde, the perfect California type, though she actually came from Philadelphia. She was a senior at Berkeley. Without in the least looking for it, I had found a sexual attraction.

Kate and I found another affinity, too—poetry. I remember that one day we rode the bus, careful not to touch knees or elbows, to hear some San Francisco poets read. I don't remember whom we heard, but they were the spawn of Patchen, Ginsberg, Ferlinghetti and Corso. One guy came out dressed in a penis costume. At first we didn't understand his mime, could not imagine what this long cloth cylinder with two globes at its feet was supposed to be. Then, as he jumped around the stage, we both blushed crimson.

After that, any tenderer approach seemed impossible, and so no approach at all was made. We rode back home in silence. Somehow something in us had been defeated, perhaps by the unbelievable extremes of our environment. A short while later Kate left to hitch back East, having felt the reins of religious authoritarianism tightening. As yet the Unified Family—it would not call itself the Unification Church until 1971—had left me plenty of slack. I remained an eager, almost puppy-like acolyte. Kirby Smith would later tell me I was so unbelievable that they feared I was a plant of some kind. Even so I felt a pang when Kate left, and I was tempted to go with her.

But the impulses that drew me into this religious commune were far stronger. I was in a frame of mind where everything proved itself, as when I broke my fast under the loquat tree. I was having many precognitions, one of the most important on a fine mid-May morning when I was knocking around on the Berkeley campus with Bobbie Devine. Bobbie was not really smart, which is to say nothing important against him. His vocabulary at times seemed less than two hundred words, but that didn't mean he couldn't teach. He was telling me about

Jesus, how he fit into the *Divine Principle*. Jesus was the son of God and the messiah, according to Moon's teaching, but for Moon there was no doctrine of a *felix culpa*, no fortunate fall. Jesus did not die to redeem man's original sin, as in orthodox Christianity. He had not been meant to die at all. He had been thwarted in his mission, which yet another messiah would now have to carry out.

It took Bobbie a long time to explain these things, but he was getting through. Here I was, learning out of the mouth of babes. I was thrilled. Booklearning was bullshit. What Bobbie had learned he had learned by rote. It was not enough, I could see, to be a Christian and believe in Christ. Salvation, I was beginning to see, was a longer, far rockier path.

There must have been a different mood on the campus that day, an evil, wicked mood. Yet we were oblivious. The first we knew of what was going on were the screams. We stopped and listened. Somewhere, thousands of people were screaming, mingling, running. We crept into a little nook between two buildings, and then, on the other side, we parted the hedge and peered out. It was Chicago all over again. Long-haired kids in jeans were getting their heads bashed by cops with riot sticks. There was a crescendo of noise and a shadow passed over us. It was a helicopter. We looked up and there were two choppers in the sky, one spraying something. Tear gas, I realized as I identified the acrid smell, but not strong enough to bother us here.

"Let's just stay here, Bobbie," I said. "It looks like we'll be fine here. Let's just go on talking."

There we sat as if in a bubble, amid evergreens, palms and bamboo, in a hedged-in grove open to the sky where the sounds of a babbling brook reached our ears. It was like Chicago, but I was no longer concerned. I was no longer a part of these great armies clashing in the distance. Those were the People's Park riots going on out there. When we returned we would learn from the news media that the police had shotgunned a number of students that day, killing one young man outright on a rooftop.

Bobbie was saying something.

"What?"

He leaned forward. His eyes were intense. The rioting had drowned out his words. He repeated them: "He is here. He is on earth. The messiah is born and he is here. Now!"

Again I was thrilled. I felt the precognition in a flash. I remembered opening a closet back in the house and finding a picture tacked up inside its door. It was of a powerful man in a kimono, a man also peaceful, wise and serene. He was Oriental, about forty, round-faced, kindly, with hooded sparkling eyes.

"Who?" I asked.

"The Reverend Moon."

But I already knew. I had already seen him. He was the man in the picture.

I spent the summer in Berkeley. I was transformed by this new life. Never was there a question of what to do with myself. From the time I rolled up and put away my sleeping bag in the morning my day was full. I had neither the time nor the inclination to flirt with the great abyss. Now I was back keeping my vow of the previous fall. I kept myself pure. In the evenings, if there was nothing else to do, no work, no witnessing, no lecturing, then we would sit in a circle and read through the *Divine Principle* aloud with Henry. One could never learn too much about the *Divine Principle*, this great writing of the master, all his teachings embodied in one great work that explained everything, heaven, hell, man, woman, God, history and the future. It was as if the Holy Bible had been written by one man.

Sometimes on Sundays we got in somebody's car—all property was regarded as more or less communal—and drove four miles to a public park in Oakland where the holy ground was.

This was ground that had been blessed by Moon himself when he had first visited the United States back in 1965. At that time he had gone to all fifty states and prayed at these given spots, where forever after his followers could come to renew their commitment and to purify themselves. When we came to these plots we were literally closer to God and to Moon as well. Here Moon had challenged Satan and called down God's power. He had laid out a sort of mandala, a diamond shape with four positions with God at the top, man and woman at each side, and children, the fruit of their consecrated love for God and each other, at the bottom.

Perhaps Moon had not gone to all fifty states. Such oral history—legend in the making—was variously reported. Sometimes it was said that Moon had visited forty states, not fifty. So there was some question as to whether there was holy ground in Alaska and Hawaii. At any rate forty represented cosmic completion. Forty was one of the many significant numbers in Moon's teaching. For instance, the Old Testament deluge had lasted forty days, Jesus had been tempted in the wilderness for forty days, King David had ruled his country for forty years, and the Israelites suffered in the wilderness for four hundred years (multiples were significant, too). These plots were laid out or marked only in the minds of Moon's followers and they were in all kinds of places. Ours was in a public park. Los Angeles' was out in the country on a hill. Washington's was on the Ellipse.

Often we would join hands and have a group prayer aloud on the holy ground. When our spiritual parents, Henry and Anne Muso, led, the prayers were particularly passionate. In fact, Henry and Anne always ended their prayers in tears. I was particularly impressed by this. I myself probably had not cried since I was thirteen.

Then when we were ready to leave, Henry would scream: "*Abo gi!*" I was told this was Korean for father.

We would all jump up in the air and throw our hands up and cry: "*Mon sei.*" I understood that this was rather like the

Japanese battle cry in World War II, *ban sei*; it meant victory for ten thousand years.

In early August an urbane Englishman named Cecil Meecham showed up. Cecil, who was tall, well read, well spoken, who epitomized the public-school-educated English upper class, was from national headquarters in Washington. He was as sophisticated as a diplomat, too, having traveled extensively. Living as he was in a foreign country now, he was on something of a diplomatic mission. I got along with him well. We had read many of the same books, particularly books on the East, mysticism and the occult (one reason I had been drawn to San Francisco was that Edgar Cayce had predicted another great earthquake there at this time and I wanted to be in on it). As much as I might convince myself I liked people like Mayer and his invisible dwarf, or Bobbie, or Bennie Sutherland, the rock singer who came to Jesus after an overjolt of acid, they didn't read books and we couldn't communicate as Cecil and I could.

Cecil said that I was prime material and that I ought to come to Washington to complete my education. In Washington there was a larger and more interesting group. There was political action, for, more than I knew at that time, Moon's teaching was wedded to action. His was no otherworldly religion. Indeed, he conceded a duality between the spirit world and the concrete objective world that the five senses perceived, but he expected his followers to have a firm foot in both worlds. Also in Washington was one of the Unified Family's saints, Miss Kim, virtually the first missionary to the North American continent, veritably the new Saint Paul, the bringer of the word.

She, I knew, had been converted in Korea long enough ago to qualify as an original disciple. She had been suffering from a terminal intestinal disease, as the story went, and had reluctantly consented, for the sake of a friend, to see this shaman-mystic-healer. Within a week of meeting Moon, she was miraculously well. Then, some ten years ago, this small, frail

woman had arrived utterly alone and with no particular resources other than her own determination, to spread the teachings of her master in America. Not that she had succeeded
to any astounding degree. At this time there were perhaps
one hundred or one hundred twenty members of the Unified
Family in the United States.

No one particularly disagreed with Cecil and within the
month I was again traveling by car across the country. This
time I picked up a ride on the Berkeley bulletin board and
made the trip in three and three-quarter days in an MG
Midget driven by a fellow who was taking a job as a statis-
tician with a congressional committee. We stopped for nine
hours in Wyoming and for six hours with friends of his farther
on and otherwise we just kept going in his little open car. By
the time we arrived our lips were as parched and cracked
as if we had crossed the Sahara on camelback.

National headquarters was at 1611 Upshur Street, N.W., a
big, funny old house with a double-pointed roof in a nice
upper-middle-class black neighborhood with lots of big, shady
maple trees. The building had once been the Libyan embassy.
I was shown to a small room among the many on the second
floor. There I would sleep on the blue close-cropped rug, because everyone in the Unified Family slept on the floor except
Miss Kim, who did not either because she was a saint or because she was older or because she was rather frail.

I had arrived during the dinner hour, and after I had brought
my stuff to the room I joined the group of twenty-five or thirty
seated at the two long cafeteria-style tables down in the lino-
leum-floored basement. Miss Kim sat at the end of one table
and I was seated next to her. I was somewhat awed by Miss
Kim. I knew her from the photograph that appeared on the
back of the early editions of the *Divine Principle*, which she
had translated. That picture showed a Korean maiden of about
thirty-two in Oriental dress. She had an oval face, even features, lovely dark eyes and a mouth full and yet disciplined.

Now I saw her some eighteen years later and she was still pretty. Her hair was still long and jet black and she wore it pinned up. What her movements and posture now showed especially, and what the portrait had not been able to convey entirely, was how feminine and graceful she was.

I don't remember what I ate that first meal, but I do remember Miss Kim's quiet, gentle exploration of my personality. She asked me many questions about myself, but never in a rude stand-and-deliver manner that I might have expected from someone who so obviously held the respect of everyone in the room. She asked about the trip and observed that I must be exhausted, wanted to know about my education, my religious background, my hopes for the future, about my family and where I was from.

"Princeton," I answered.

"I thought that was a university." Her English was precise, pronounced delicately.

"It is. It is also a nice town. Many people are confused by that."

"It is not so far from here?"

"No, not at all."

"Will you visit your parents?"

"Yes, of course. We are a close family. I have not seen them for four months."

"You have not seen them since you joined us?"

"No."

"Have you written them?"

"Yes."

"What do they say?"

"They don't really seem to understand. But this has been a rather confusing time for us. They will."

"They may not. I would not be surprised, Allen, if they never do. Most of us here are not old like me, but young. Many times families are the enemies of religious experience. Jesus said: 'For I am come to set man at variance against his father. A man's foes shall be they of his own household. He that loveth father or mother more than me is not worthy of me.' Be prepared for the worst. Your family will oppose you in this. They will try to take you from us."

This was not the first time nor the last time I would hear such sentiments. I had heard them many times already at Berkeley. We had been a young group, nearly all in our way dropouts, some of us deeply hurt, even maimed by the conflict with our society, and tales of ferocious fights with parents were commonplace.

That night I looked down the rows of faces and there were many smiles for me. Like the Berkeley group, they were delighted to welcome newcomers. In the weeks and months that followed, I would come to know them all. At the head of the table were Frank and Elise Lyons, the spiritual leaders under Miss Kim. They were the head of this group and of the whole American family, and they represented Adam and Eve on the way to restoration to their prelapsarian powers. Then there was Jeff Shaw, a balding printer of about thirty-eight, and his wife Amelia, a few years younger and pathologically skinny, for she had an extreme anorexia and vomited up nearly everything she ate. Carl Beck was nervous about newcomers and had been with Miss Kim nearly from the beginning ten years before. He was shy, a blusher, convinced at age thirty-six that he was a failure. His wife Sharon was idealistic, pretty, well educated, and well read.

Among the single females in the group was Becky Boyd, another long-termer who at twenty-nine or so was a powerful force in the movement. Jean Finch was thirty and a speech major at American University. Bernadine Stoller was in her late twenties and was a photographer for a magazine within a federal agency. Beth Adams was the group's only black; she was twenty-three and worked for a small suburban newspaper. Toby Moran had turned from the Hare Krishnas in her mid-twenties and she had a secretarial job.

One of the most forceful males was Neil Salonen, who

looked, acted and dressed like an Ivy Leaguer gone into sales. He headed the political arm of the family, called the Freedom Leadership Foundation. Miles Taylor had been born a Methodist and had converted to Judaism at age nineteen. Now he was twenty-two, without a degree, but artistic and self-consciously brilliant. He was something of a little Hitler type, overbearing to say the least. His manner must have served him well in his work, which had been in theater. He did theater design, acted, and had directed many plays. He told me that he gave up the theater because you had to be a homosexual to succeed.

Beatrice Owens had been a Franciscan nun for twenty years. She had fallen in love with a priest and in the subsequent crisis had come into contact with the Unified Family. She had gone back and tried to convert the other nuns, telling them that the messiah was here on earth now. The convent sent her for psychiatric testing, found her sane, and so booted her out. Now at age forty-five she had a job in town, a little green car, and she was particularly friendly with me because she had taken my grandfather's course when he taught at the writing seminars at the University of Minnesota, back in the days when the Catholic Church was sending its soldiers to study with the Great Catholic Thinker.

Waldo McKane was only eighteen and had arrived one day from St. Louis on a big Harley and stayed. Richard Lind had come with a dog; he stayed and the dog went. He was told to let people who have less important things to do keep pets.

Like many of the young males, Mark Tillman had no job, but he picked up work when he could and helped Jeff the printer when he couldn't. He was asthmatic, but spunky and nice, despite the fact that he was often made the butt of jokes. Confirming the pattern of older, better-educated females with paying jobs was Elsa Reiner, who spoke German, Spanish and English. She had founded the Columbia Heights day-care center, which was largely for black and Hispanic mothers and which was funded with a $100,000 federal grant. Elsa was twenty-seven. She was a good source of low-level pickup jobs, for, as director of the center, she was in charge of hiring.

Jerome Williams was a thirty-two-year-old ex-Air Force man who spoke fluent Russian and now translated for the Defense Department. Millicent Schultz was nearing thirty and was moving along in a career as a psychiatric social worker. The group included three more young men in their early twenties: Cecil Meecham; Horace Burbank, a Midwesterner who had a civil service job; and Simon Morris, a gregarious athlete who was a senior at Georgetown.

Life in the center was communal, in everything but sex and money. It would be two years before all financial assets were collectivized. If they had jobs, people were encouraged to keep them, and if they didn't, work was found for them, paying or nonpaying. Resources and property, which, generally speaking, meant motor vehicles, were grudgingly shared.

I could see right away that the blissful Berkeley days were gone. The Washington center was busy, businesslike, and the work went on along two fronts, religious and political. Ironically, there had been no politics for us in Berkeley, though it was in the eye of the storm as far as the politics of the nation's youth went.

Here began my political education. The hard fact was that Reverend Moon was an utter hawk, totally for the Vietnam war and for America's armed intervention. The whole latter part of the *Divine Principle* dealt with politics and history and Moon taught that the third world war was inevitable. History moved ahead by a dialectic and at this point stood poised for the final synthesis, which would culminate in the final holocaust, the final judgment, the third and final world war and the second and final coming. On one side were good, Abel, God, democracy and Moon. On the other side were Cain, Satan and communism. The final reconciliation could come about in one of two ways, through conviction (ideological battle) or through force (literal battle). What was settled ideologically would be settled peacefully. But those who did not come along willingly would be scourged with the worldly arsenal of napalm and nukes.

Accepting this required a complete ideological flip-flop for me. Not much more than a year ago I had stood on the steps of the burned-out ROTC building at Sewanee and made an antiwar speech befitting an SDS standard bearer. Yet now I was making a tight 180-degree turn on the war issue, and furthermore, it didn't seem to be causing any vibration or strain. I explained this ideological dime-turn by telling myself that previously I had had only a small piece of the whole picture. Now, with the opening of my spiritual eye, came a far more complete view. One thing remained constant, though. After McCarthy, Chicago, a couple of years of youth politics, marches and demonstrations, America was turning around on the Vietnam war. But I remained, now as much as that time on the steps of the ROTC building, on the decidedly unpopular side of the issue.

Since I had only a part-time job, I worked with Neil Salonen with the Freedom Leadership Foundation. This was the toned-down name for the organization that was known elsewhere—in Korea, Japan and in certain European countries, for Moon was gaining ground with disaffected youth along an international front—as the International Foundation for the Extermination of Communism.

My mother had pulled strings to get me a part-time job with our home district's good-guy antiwar congressman, Frank Thompson, whom she had helped to reelect several times. I worked for Thompy from ten to three for $289 a month, and did the footwork, picked things up, ran messages, fetched coffee, went to change $100 bills and when nothing important like that was needed, sat in on committees to report back to his aides what, for instance, the congressional committee on the Smithsonian Institution was doing about next year. When nothing at all was going on, I sat around drinking coffee and trying to convert the secretaries. Working for an antiwar congressman was a bizarre contrast with the rest of my life, which these days involved proselytizing for the war on the American University campus, to which Salonen had assigned me.

After work I would come back to the big Upshur Street house, where members from all over the country were holding meetings during the FLF's second United States conference. We were assigned projects, met in seminars, wrote and read papers concerning such topics as why there is so much violence in the peace movement and what the communist and Marxist point of view was. We discussed the Panthers and other radicals and came to our own conclusions about the *Divine Principle* solution to world politics.

Salonen was hooked up with two very interesting Washingtonians who gave him a great deal of help on political action. They were Foster Long, a former aide to Senator Thomas Dodd and a former staffer on the infamous Internal Security Committee, and Marshall Miller, who was formerly in the Peace Corps or the State Department stationed in Peru or Chile. Miller was in his early thirties, had a degree in history or literature from UCLA or USC and wore tweed suits, rep ties and Bass Weejun loafers.

Miller was a patriot, and the basis of his patriotism was patriotism. He was different from Long, who claimed to have once been a Red, and who had paled over Stalin's atrocities, or so the story went. Miller went to monthly luncheons where he probably met with old McCarthy types—the bad McCarthy from Wisconsin—and he had a paper organization called the United Student Alliance, which actually existed only on four or five campuses, mainly local ones. He claimed it was a national organization, and later he would use names of Unified Family members from everywhere on his letterhead to try to make good this dubious assertion. Best of all, Marshall was independently wealthy and had all the time and money he needed to devote to his causes. He was just too damned perfect. It never occurred to me then, but later I wondered if he was a fed, an FBI or CIA covert agent.

There were many rooms with sliding doors in the Upshur Street house, and Marshall and Foster and Neil were always sidling into one of them for high-level meetings I was not invited to. I envied them.

In October we stepped up our action to coincide with the national moratoriums against the war slated for October 15 and November 15. Several of us joined forces with some Young Americans for Freedom and held a three-day pro-war fast on the Ellipse. The POWs were the best means of wrenching sentiment from the issue, we learned, and I believe it was Foster Long who helped us to get some U.S. Information Agency atrocity pictures to blow up for display. I remember one particularly: the heads of five G.I.'s sitting on the ground like pumpkins after the harvest.

The Washington press covered the fast, but the reporters, possibly because the Unified Family was an unknown quantity at the time, ended up giving all the credit to the YAFers, who were by far in the minority. I was now the veteran of several three- and four-day fasts, though I had not yet done the big seven-day one, which was required if you were going the whole course. Becky Boyd was finishing up her long one, and I well remember her vomiting when we broke the fast with pig fat and pumpkin soup, which is what we were told the POWs ate.

My parents did not yet really understand what was going on with me. I had visited briefly, but they had only a vague idea that I was into yoga, self-realization and fellowship, more of what I had been drifting toward since Sewanee. The name Moon as yet meant nothing to them. Flo, however, with whom I had dinner one evening, immediately grasped what was going on. She flatly told me that I was throwing my life away.

By October 15 I was telling my parents that the peace movement had been infiltrated by the communists. When my parents came down to Washington on November 15 for the moratorium, I refused to march with them. This, more than anything that had happened yet, upset them. The war, even now that she had gotten her sons out, was a dear issue to my mother. She concluded that I was taken in by some kind of right-wing "front."

The fundamental stuff did not hit the fan until Christmas, however. If indeed I maintain a certain distance and diffidence in the retelling of my story, it is difficult to communicate how devoted I was to my new religion and cause. People tell me of my zombie-like countenance at the time. I had no sense of it. Possibly I seemed to others like members of the Progressive Labor Party seemed to me. I was as passionately involved in Moon's system as any paranoiac could be in his. I could think of little else and it colored all of my perceptions.

So that Christmas I brought a copy of the *Divine Principle* up to Princeton. My mother read it. Indeed, she critiqued it. She underlined, scribbled marginalia and, when we were seated around the living-room fireplace, she hurled her rebuttals. This stuff was pig's swill to her. She quoted against it all the Catholic theologians she knew, and she was well read in Maritain and the other modern ones. Perhaps if this had been an intellectual debate I would have been devastated. But it wasn't an intellectual debate. It was a sheer contest of wills. And on that naked level I was determined not to lose. In the end she grew verbally violent, abusive, hysterical. It was the worst thing she could have done. It stiffened my resolve.

Perhaps it didn't really matter after my mother had taken her tack, but my father took the other one, and he would maintain it during my whole stint in the Unified Family. He took a hands-off, detached attitude. He could hardly have been more professional with one of his own patients.

The exception was one particular little mental judo chop he managed to deal me from behind, when I wasn't looking or expecting it. One late afternoon or early evening of one of the string of Christmas parties at Hodge Road, my father asked me to explain Moon's doctrine that adultery was the original sin. I dutifully launched into it, cold sober myself, as seriously as if I was witnessing back in the wilds of Dupont Circle. With a deft remark that I have now forgotten, my father brought the house down laughing at me.

Laughter of that kind is as exquisite as a public flogging. It showed what a master of manipulation my father could be. It would have been bad enough if he alone had laughed at me, but he had set his many-toothed trap, led me along the path, and then sprung it.

I returned to Washington utterly humiliated.

Miss Kim had predicted all this. The power of prediction was the power of prophecy: she must be correct, divinely inspired at least. This also confirmed my commitment.

Yet for all that I was wavering. The way in which I was wavering is a subtle yet important point. Freud tells us that in dreams yes can mean yes or no, just as no can mean yes or no. In dreams the crossroads are more important than which fork you take, negative or positive. I had already flipped from anti-war to pro-war without any period of reasonable transition, and presumably I might as well go back again. You can, in the course of a heated argument, most passionately defend a point at the very moment you begin to have doubts that you are correct. A married couple can be most passionately committed just before the breakup. Beneath my devotion to Moon there was an uneasiness that I would scarcely allow into my consciousness.

For one thing, the spiritual work in Washington, unlike that in Berkeley, was going badly. Our restored Adam, Frank Lyons, was in some kind of difficulty. Rumors were going around that his marriage with Elise was troubled. It was whispered that he was "possessed by homosexual spirits." Old gossip was revived about how he once had planned to run away with another young male in the center.

The failure of leadership was felt. I felt it, though actually I liked Frank personally. He was a sensitive soul, I could see, and though he was uneducated, he was something of an artist.

He liked me, and I remembered that he had given me thirty-five dollars to buy a pair of shoes. Once he had told me about how he had had some kind of Jesus experience when he was in the army in Korea. He had been in the church for a long time, and he and Elise were among the first American couples to be "blessed," or married, by Moon during his second visit to America in 1969. They were to have been the original root of the American branch, eventually fructifying and having children—of which so far there was no sign—and standing in as the spiritual parents of the new converts, like me.

Miss Kim, our saint, took no action that we could see. She watched and waited. And then, as if to prove the old Oriental adage that all things come to she who waits, the situation resolved itself. The right answer was apparent. Frank cracked up. He took a weepy farewell from us one evening at dinner, and then he and Elise went to Boston, where a new center was in the bud and where he was expected to pull himself and his marriage together.

Meanwhile I went to Miss Kim and told her I was thinking of going back to finish my degree. Undoubtedly she sensed my ambivalence, and she in turn manifested her own two minds. Ordinarily she would be happy that I was returning to college. The family liked to have its members take all possible degrees, diplomas, prizes and credits, but she shrewdly guessed that if I moved into another milieu, they might well lose me. It was decided I should go to Mona the medium, Mona the mind reader, for the answer.

Already I had heard a great deal about Mona, and soon I would know more. She was one of the most colorful figures who had ever lived in the Washington center. She had moved out, but she had kept a unique and privileged relationship with the Unified Family.

Mona was a former Olympic contender in the women's shot put, discus and javelin. No doubt she had always been a big woman, but now she was enormous, weighing over three hundred pounds, possibly even more. Her bulk defied my capacity to estimate. She was the daughter of an Oregon all-American, and now, still in her early twenties, she had founded, headed and still coached a track team for black kids out of the Washington ghetto, and she was beloved of the inner-city community for all the athletic scholarships she helped its children get.

Many of our people were afraid of Mona. She could look into people's eyes and tell whether they were lying. There were many stories of her astounding people by mind reading. Almost everyone has heard such stories about somebody, and I believed the ones about her. In personality she was like an honest, self-righteous child, which, in combination with her extrasensory perceptions, was like nitro-glycerin. She could reputedly obliterate people, leaving them nothing much more than a crater of their former selves. Mona was beyond the dogmas and codes of the Unified Family; moreover, she defied them fearlessly, even, to a degree, the sexual ones. She often played a kind of mock pretty-girl role, bizarre considering her mammoth girth, in which she was very huggy-kissy and even patted asses. Such behavior was an absolute no-no for anyone else in the Family.

"Go pray with her," said Miss Kim. "You will receive an answer."

I phoned her up and was told to come right over.

She lived in a three-room apartment on the tenth floor of an apartment building on 16th Street in northwest Washington. Mona had blue-green eyes and a rather pink face; she wore a jet-black sort of pooped-up and sprayed-in-place hairdo, offset with earrings. She wore makeup and dressed femininely, with care.

We took to each other. After we had talked awhile she told me I had spiritual powers, and that I should heed them. She told me how she first discovered her own powers: "I saw a spot of light," she said, "and it grew and grew until it obliterated all vision." All normal vision, that is. Now she could leave her body, that great corporeal hindrance and anchor, and travel freely in astral regions, where she could converse with spirits.

We knelt on her living-room rug and prayed. Her prayer was simple. Mona asked that she once again would be granted her powers, that she would be taught to use them for good and for the love of others. I asked for direction and guidance, and I asked that I be granted the will to follow the right path when it was clear and that I not be swayed by self-interest.

"I see a star over your head," Mona said as I prepared to leave. "It is a sign of kingship. You are destined to rule." She also told me to finish college: "All these illiterates will be dropped by the wayside when things really get rolling." I left with the sense that I had made an important and influential friend. I liked Mona and I sensed in her a genuine humility.

Within a few weeks a shake-up was in progress. The organization's new president—who was neither elected nor appointed, but chosen by an indefinite in-between process (which might even include consultations with Mona in her role as medium)—was Kirby Smith from Berkeley. I was glad; Kirby was my friend. But others, especially those who might also be considered strong contenders for leadership, like Neil Salonen, were not so glad. Kirby, I sensed after watching him a few weeks, would have been delighted to rule like a beloved saint, like Mohandas Gandhi, with no need of the trappings of power.

He failed to build up a coterie of friends. By and large Kirby couldn't tell who his friends were. He envied someone like Salonen, who was an operator and who could even get his enemies to work for him. Consequently, very shortly thereafter, Kirby became isolated. When he saw that he was losing control over the situation, he engineered a shake-up and hoped that when the dust settled things would be more to his liking. Kirby decided it was time to send out some missionaries.

Elsa, a strong personality who would have been willing to back Kirby to the hilt if he had only known it, was to be sent to St. Louis to start another center. And, most important of the new assignments, Salonen would go take the word to Colorado. But this would leave open the ever-so-important job of heading the Freedom Leadership Foundation.

I well remember the day a long-faced Salonen came to me and said he was going away for a while and asked would I like, would I be able, to run the FLF while he was gone.

"Gee, I guess so," I answered, as befitted an organizational ingenue. I had been ill for four days and was lying on the living-room floor in my sleeping bag. I was weak.

Neil said he would write Moon in Korea that I would be running the political arm of the church while he was gone. I understood that this was a temporary arrangement and that at some indefinite time Salonen would be returning.

What I didn't tell Neil, however, was that I already knew I was going to head the FLF. Word had come from Mona, who presumably had gotten the word during her astral out-of-the-body travels. Kirby later discovered that I had found out a week and a half earlier from Mona, whom he accused of trying to subvert his leadership. A lasting rift developed between those two, but it was no more important than many others. They were wielding power, such as it was, in an organization in which the mantle of leadership was settled on this or that person not by election or any other orderly procedure, but rather by whim, intrigue and extrasensory perception.

So at the tender age of twenty-two I found myself at the head of the most important organization within the Unified Family. I was the second-highest-ranking member, after Kirby Smith—third really, if I counted Miss Kim, who was fading at this time. After over a decade of missionary work, she was clearly growing weary. For me, it wasn't like being sent to the United Nations, but neither was heading the FLF, as I was to discover, exactly like being in the student government or the absolute bush leagues.

With Foster Long and Marshall Miller to advise me, I quickly learned the art of being a paper tiger with a real roar. Marshall's eyes would glaze over whenever the ideological stuff was discussed, but he would perk up for the practical applications. He had considerable contacts, including some top-level hookups in the Nixon administration. It was through him that I met two of Nixon's top aides on Vietnam, Dolph Droge and Sven Kramer.

In May 1970, Marshall and I formed a lobby, which we registered as the American Youth for a Just Peace. Its members were the members of the Unified Family. One of our professed goals was to defeat the Cooper-Church and the McGovern-Hatfield amendments, which were aiming, especially in the wake of the Cambodian invasion of March 1970, to cut off funding for the Vietnam war.

That legislation also proposed a cutoff of military aid to Israel, and for that reason we were able to form a coalition with another group, a Jewish one called the Youth Committee for Peace and Democracy in the Middle East, or the YCPDME, pronounced Yicpidimee. I remember some huddles with some young Jews and a bald professor from American University in which we discussed world affairs over coffee and bagels. Yicpidimee was even more of a paper organization than our AYJP, and so we loaned them some FLF names for their board and some of our other members across the country so they also could appear to be a large national organization.

That spring some of our people, wearing red FLF armbands, held a teach-in at American U. with Yicpidimee, and it ended up with a lot of near fights with the Arab students. Except for that, our coalition never came to anything, for the simple reason that the young Jews were hot on one issue only, Israel, and would not take a hawk stance on Vietnam.

After that the American Youth for a Just Peace stood absolutely alone. We were virtually the only pro-war lobby in Washington. Perhaps it is not surprising, then, that our link with the Nixon administration strengthened. Word came through Marshall Miller that even higher aides wanted to see us. During this time I went over to the Executive Office Building, whose long polished marble floors and hushed hallways reminded me of nothing so much as a high-school building during summer vacation, to meet Jeb Stuart Magruder and Charles Colson, whom I remember most vividly of the two. He was a froglike man with a squashed nose and strange eyebrows that went around the sides of his face.

"Why don't you boys come on inside?" Colson asked, clearly meaning that we should work directly for the White House. We declined.

One day about this time Marshall showed me a cashier's check for several thousand dollars.

"This is from Colson," he said. "It's not from the President. It's from 'friends of the President.' Remember that. Or else our source could quickly dry up."

We used the money to open an office down in the Washington business district, at 13th and H Streets, N.W. We rented a suite on the top floor of a nice solid Washington high-rise built after the turn of the century. Marshall and I each had a paneled private office; our two secretaries sat together in another room. We also paid ourselves little salaries —I think mine was $85 a week—which was enough for me to buy a suit or two and take people out to lunch occasionally.

Our secretaries were women from the center, Becky Boyd, who had worked for Salonen when he headed the FLF, and Elizabeth Burns, a beauty with long blond hair. They drew tiny little salaries, too, though they were both crack secretaries. Becky never made a mistake. She was a friend of Salonen's—later she would marry him—and she was afraid that I would supplant him. She was well aware that things were zipping along in the FLF as they never had under him and she wouldn't like anybody to think that the difference lay in my talents or his lack of them.

I was also aware that many people back in the center, including President Smith himself, were becoming jealous of me. While they were back holding prayer meetings and buttonholing prospective converts, I was in the limelight, talking to Colson, going out to lunch with professors, savoring every atmospheric whiff of cloak, dagger, romance and adventure. Becky, I learned, was reporting back that I was being eaten away by Pride, and she was finding ready listeners.

Elizabeth was a danger of quite a different order. I think both Marshall and I were somewhat in love with her. Her good looks had caused trouble before. That had been with Frank Lyons' predecessor as head of the family, a story which also revealed why Miss Kim was so tired and how the early course of the Unified Family had been anything but smooth. In this fellow, whose name has now been expunged from messianic history, God's word apparently shortcircuited and the sexual prohibition reversed poles so that it came out that the Lord *wanted* him to sleep with all of these women. Elizabeth was one of them, the only participant in these satanic goings-on who had not been expelled from the Unified Family, apparently because in her case there was some mitigating circumstance.

It was, of course, Satan who had shortcircuited God's word and sabotaged Moon's early mission to America. We believed in Satan as much as any Baptist or fundamentalist, perhaps more, and we knew that if the prayers were left unsaid, if the indemnities of hard work, fasting and selflessness were not paid, then Satan could step in and seize our work.

Elizabeth had been almost crushed in the aftermath of this catastrophe and only now, after several years, was she beginning to flicker back to life. Miss Kim still treated her with utter contempt.

Elizabeth, incidentally, had come into the fold by an unusual route. She had not been converted by Miss Kim nor even by one of Miss Kim's converts, but by Col. Bo Hi Pak, who was a former South Korean military attaché. This was back in 1963 or 1964, after Pak had formed a close relationship with Moon in Korea, and when he was back in Washington as a sort of cultural emissary, as the head of the Korean and Cultural Freedom Foundation. Pak now did things like arrange a year-long United States tour for a Korean children's dance group, the Little Angels, and he knew all the ropes in Washington. In his long career there he seemed to have been photographed shaking hands with every Washington celebrity, from President Eisenhower on down (none of whom had the slightest inkling he was to become the emissary of a new messiah).

Certainly Pak—a tall, slender, polite man with an erect military bearing, who wore a black Chesterfield overcoat with a white silk scarf—was a familiar figure over on Upshur Street. Yet there was still an enmity between Col. Pak and Miss Kim, apparently stemming from the time when Reverend Moon had considered installing him in Miss Kim's position. At times it seemed that the Reverend Moon resented having a female Saint Paul. At any rate, Pak's and Kim's animosity was well cloaked now, especially by Pak, who was perfectly capable of such deceptions as pretending he knew less English than he did when it suited him. In converting Elizabeth, he had forgotten to tell her that Moon was the messiah, but she joined anyway.

Chairman Wood and Chairman Miller sat in their offices and every two weeks put out a little tabloid newsletter, four pages when folded, which we mailed out to members of Congress, schools, libraries, organizations, embassies and whomever else was not likely to throw it away. We gleaned our information on Southeast Asia from the daily press, from the U.S. Information Agency, from the Vietnamese and Cambodian embassies—which is to say we had nothing new. Our twist—and here I was learning the art of propagandizing in a classic situation—was that we had a consistent theoretical position. Essentially we were just putting a slant on the news that everyone knew.

As we said in one issue of the paper, which was printed by photo offset in blue with photographs: "AYJP is a private nonpartisan organization comprised of students and young people committed not only to peace, but to a *just* peace, to peace with freedom, to a peace which will not reward aggression and thereby foster future wars." On the back we asked for contributions and volunteer workers, and offered to send more information. (We were building up a mailing list of several thousand.) In a box at the bottom we noted that the paper was "published by the Freedom Leadership Foundation. It seeks to promote understanding of the nature of communism, to stimulate discussion of problems in America, and to serve as an exchange of information between local chapters."

The Unified Family brought in some of its seventy-five foot-sloggers from all over the country and put them to work for the AYJP. Mainly their job was to look like good American youths and go canvass members of Congress. Congress would think a pro-war groundswell was undulating across the country. This was the stuff, *action*—no babble about Cain and Abel and Satan—which energized Marshall in manic bursts of speed.

Also in keeping with our aims as a classic front organization, we took out full-page ads in the *Washington Post* and in the *Washington Star*, stating our position and asking for contributions. The ads were good publicity, and this alone was worth the price, which hovered around $2,500 a shot. However, with the hundreds of little checks that trickled into the office after each ad—we took out three or four over a period of two months—we cleared about eight thousand dollars in all.

Marshall was a splendid teacher. He was also good at keeping our foot soldiers amused. One wonderful character he dug up to lecture for us was Willie Gee, who had been President Diem's guerrilla warfare expert. Willie would drive over to Upshur Street in a fast sports car accompanied by a fierce dog and a flashy girl. He wore a sort of black jump suit and reflector-type sunglasses which he never took off, except now and then to rub his eyes, which were bloodshot and somehow disappointingly small. (What did we expect? Tiger eyes?)

Willie would tell us what it was like to fight the VC and what it was really like in Red China. He was of medium height, somewhere between forty and fifty years old and powerfully built, with a great bullish neck. He was a karate expert, of course, and when he talked, shoveling out the anticommunist fodder for us to chew over, he was fond of making death gestures. He loved to gouge, punch, strangle and chop the air in front of him, and we could vividly imagine the fate of his victims, crumpling to the ground with shattered faces, broken backs, and paralyzed limbs.

Willie was pure macho and apparently completely worldly, though possibly it was an ascetic streak that made him refuse all food after four P.M. Otherwise, he said, he would not sleep well. Unlike Marshall and Foster Long and some others, he was not embarrassed by our religiosity. Either that or he was far more diplomatic than they.

"I once tried to make up a religion of my own," he told us once. "Your religion is the closest I have ever found to that one. That is because you believe in God and you are against the communists."

Marshall had a big house in upstate New York, and several of us—I, Foster Long, Willie Gee and others—would go up with him for philosophic anticommunist weekends. There we swam in the lake just down the slope from the house, which was full of family knickknacks. Often we cooked outside, roasting weenies as the sun set over the rolling hills. Foster would tell us, for instance, about how after he stopped being a Red he had helped refugees escape from behind the Iron Curtain.

Now that Dodd had been censured by the Senate for misuse of campaign funds, Foster, who was in his mid-fifties, was floating. He had his uses, though. He did not, like Marshall, know the ins and outs of fronting, nor did he have Marshall's links with the administration. But he did have splendid diplomatic contacts from his years advising Dodd, who was on the Foreign Affairs Committee. Those contacts, coupled with our hard pro-war labors, our cozying up to the Nixon administration which was then Vietnamizing the war, brought us a most delightful invitation. In mid-July the South Vietnamese ambassador invited me, Marshall and other members of the FLF, about a dozen in all, to a fifteen-day, all-expense-paid VIP tour of South Vietnam. We were going on a junket!

In late August 1970 we went to Dulles Airport, got interviewed by a pretty Oriental-American television reporter, and boarded a Northwest Orient Boeing 747 for Seattle, Tokyo and Hong Kong, where we laid over. Marshall had brought two of his people from the United Student Alliance, and the FLF group included our secretaries, Becky and Elizabeth; Neil Salonen, back from Denver for this; Cecil Meecham; and Miles Taylor. Kirby Smith, because of some strange quirk, or pique, chose not to come.

Marshall's boys turned out to be ever so different from us. They were cigar-smoking whore-hoppers and they knew how to conduct themselves on a junket. By Hong Kong they were already waist deep in the brothels. Our people were deeply upset by their behavior, fearing Satan would seize this enterprise. I asked Marshall to tell them to cool it, which they did. God's work could not go on in such an atmosphere.

We were greeted at the Saigon Airport by young people, male and female, from the South Vietnamese Department of the Interior, and they also appeared to have their expectations of junkets. I clearly got the idea that the girls were provided for our sexual pleasure and that they were puzzled when we didn't take advantage of them. After all, they must have wondered, were these really Americans who got off the plane and then failed to ask first, where are your women, and second, where are your raw materials?

After our picture was taken under the welcome banner, we were taken to our hotel by a bus led by a military jeep with a wailing siren. The hotel was a luxurious French colonial leftover, with a restaurant on the roof. Saigon was a shock: noisier than New York City, full of buzzing motorbikes and seething with pedestrians, lots of them pretty prostitutes in slit skirts. We were treated right away to lots of soft drinks and snacks, and diplomacy, I was to discover, involved a lot of eating. We were served sweets; honey-smothered pastry with nuts, much like baklava; meats, including chicken, in what appeared to be seaweed; and lots of rice and soy sauce. In a way it was fortunate that I got a wrenching bowel upset, despite my care not to drink the water: otherwise I might have gained even more weight than I did.

The next day three of the five big daily newspapers attacked us as lackeys of Agnew, which seemed to me proof that Thieu's regime was still a democracy. I felt that such freedom of the press would not have been permitted in the United States during World War II, when America, the very guardian of liberty, shackled the press.

We began a round of visits to leaders—leaders of all kinds: opposition leaders, labor leaders, student leaders—all the while shadowed by a Vietnamese colonel (sometimes, but not always, the same man). The attitude of all of these people was strange. They seemed to see us and yet not see us. I began to realize that they didn't really expect us to understand. They believed the situation was really too complicated for them to be able to explain it to us. Even if you said you understood, they knew you didn't. They would nod politely, always they were deferential and gentle about it, but you could see that they didn't believe you.

I was relieved when we headed out for four or five days upcountry. We did official things, like putting wreaths on the graves of those massacred at Hue, but the pleasures of this part of the trip were those of being a simple tourist. For me, visiting the Far East was the fulfillment of a dream. I was delighted to see a Buddhist monk who had been meditating under the same palm tree for seventeen years. I was transported back to the time of my readings in Eastern mysticism a few years ago. How eagerly I would have wished to question just such a man, if I had the time and if he could reply. What wisdom he must have, this man with his shaved head and saffron robe, growing old under a tree that was slowly growing larger.

At a monastery I spoke to the senior monk. I tried to draw him out. I told him that we also were seekers after God and wisdom.

"What is the difference between Christ and Buddha?" I asked him.

"None."

"When is Christ returning to Earth?"

"Now."

And then he said, through our interpreter, that if I was really a seeker I should remain with him. I explained that a few years ago I would have been delighted with his offer, but now things had changed. His eyes, as I took my leave, remained quite blank, utterly unreadable. I was often to wonder, was this invitation really meant or were we indeed just making diplomatic small talk?

We met more leaders, the leaders of six or seven villages. One village was said to be a two-thousand-year-old democracy where the art of self-determination had long been practiced. The saying here was, we were told, that the emperor's rule ended at the village gates. We also met with a local military leader, an ARVN leader and an American advisor. We visited temples, saw karate demonstrations, spent nights in the jungle, when we got down to the Mekong River, in well-guarded huts, and went to a military college at Dalat, a beautiful mountain town. As much as anything, I remember a picnic by a waterfall where two baby elephants were tied to a tree.

We returned to Saigon. It was hot, hotter even than Tennessee. The temperature seemed to hover around one hundred degrees, day and night. Something was heating up between Elizabeth and me, too. When possible, traveling on buses on tours or seated and listening to this or that leader, we chose to sit next to each other, like sweethearts in the seventh grade. It was not much more than that. Now and then our arms brushed. Back at the hotel, the room Marshall and I shared was right next to hers, and we had a balcony in common. A couple of times, during sleepless tropical nights, we stood out there alone together, overlooking the lights of what had to be at this time, with so many strange and contradictory forces at work within it, the most absolutely exotic city on earth. There was nothing explicit in this, certainly no explicit sex, no explicit touching, except for the brushing and the one time I put my arm around her on a chilly mountain morning in a Jeep, not really even any explicit talk. We just talked about everyday things, while we looked into one another's eyes.

Finally our group was led behind the presidential palace to a sort of backyard where I recall a structure which may have been a little house or maybe a trailer, but it definitely had a fold-up-and-take-away sense about it. There, standing on the steps to the doorway, was President Nguyen Van Thieu, wearing slacks and a shirt open at the neck. He was a short man, stocky but not fat, and gracious and courtly as we were each in turn introduced. He offered us drinks, which he mixed personally, and we accepted them, though in fact we never otherwise drank. I had a light bourbon and water, my first in years. For him, surely, dealing in this social ritual was an acquired diplomatic grace, as if an American emissary in Japan had learned to pour tea and bow and hobble around on his knees, and we must have realized he could scarcely relate to us as Americans if we did not sit around him in a semicircle holding glasses of booze with gently clinking ice cubes.

We talked about the usual topics, what would be expected in the circumstances, about the United States' presence in Vietnam, the good and the bad of it, and about the country in general. Then Thieu went off on a tangent about the white man, the little boy and the buffalo. While I understood every word that Thieu said, and while the story obviously had a metaphorical meaning, I never did feel I fully fathomed its meaning. Perhaps the anecdote just didn't translate into English, which Thieu spoke very well. It seems that when he was a little boy Thieu had herded water buffalo. Little boys herding these beasts—asleep, in fact, on their great flat backs, three barrels wide—were a common sight all through Vietnam. Thieu had learned that the smell of a white man would drive these crescent-horned buffalo mad, because the white man was an animal the black buffalo had never seen. But a little fifty-pound Vietnamese boy with a switch had no trouble controlling the buffalo, which must have weighed nearly a ton.

When our tour was almost over an invitation came from the Congress of Cambodian Intellectuals for a similar but shorter VIP tour of Cambodia, and we accepted. That worked out especially well for those of us, myself included, who were going on to attend the World Anticommunist League Conference in Japan in a few weeks. As long as we were finagling airline passages, we might as well do what needed doing over here. Another group, Kirby Smith included, was going to Korea, where Moon was going to marry hundreds of couples, and I was going to Korea, too, to meet Moon, although I had no marriage prospect. If I had known then how apparently impulsively Moon matched up noses for blessed couples, I might have been worried about Elizabeth's and my flirtation, because in the Unified Family there was no ritual of courtship and Moon was perfectly capable of marrying couples who had not even known each other a day or two before. This was not so strange to Koreans and Japanese, who were accustomed to having their marriages arranged.

Before we left Vietnam, however, we called a press conference. We held it at the Press Club, and hundreds of reporters turned out to hear our story and take our handout. The press, though I did not realize it then, had heard what we had to say many times from many sources. It was, in fact, the official line. The press didn't want to hear it again and they asked us questions about things we weren't prepared to discuss. The worst reporters, from our point of view, were the Europeans, who treated us like fascists or racketeers. We were unsettled by this flop of a press conference, but we were bolstered by the thought that truly we were neither right nor left but actually believed in a third position, so far hidden: Moon's. Within a few weeks I would know a great deal more about that position.

Our takeoff from Tan Son Nhut Airport was delayed by about three hours and so we were quite late in arriving at the Phnom Penh airport. Still, we were greeted by a crowd, including two lines each of fifty high-school girls holding bouquets of flowers, which they gave us to take back to the hotel. The students who met us were not junket-wise, like the Vietnamese, and these girls, with their doe-like eyes, radiated a guileless, sexless innocence that reminded me of people out of Kipling's *The Jungle Book*.

I found Cambodia more exotic, more Buddhist than Vietnam. We were able to move around freely in Phnom Penh and we appeared to be entirely welcome, which was not the feeling we had gotten in Saigon. The inner city seemed untouched by the war—Nixon's "incursion" had been only a few months earlier—and where Saigon roared along in the din of motorbikes and cars, Phnom Penh purred along almost silently. Its people traveled by rickshaw and bicycle. Yet in another way the war was closer, quite literally. All day and half the night we could hear the sounds of fighting out on the perimeter of the city: single shots, the thump of a mortar, an occasional burst of machine-gun fire. We met students who wore black pajamas and went out to the perimeter in the mornings in school buses and fought with far, far outdated equipment. We were not able to travel as much outside the city, either. The country was simply not as secure as South Vietnam. Everywhere in this city, too, we felt the presence of the colonial French, indirectly, through the palatial architecture they had left behind. Here, I again often had the feeling of being in a high-school building during summer vacation.

Again we met leaders—among the military ones, Sirik Matak, and another general who was a cousin of the exiled Prince Sihanouk. This general was now against his cousin, who he said was inviting the Reds in, and he said that without Nixon's invasion the country would have fallen within weeks. He said the country was now dependent on the United States, which he didn't like, but it was a fact. He said he looked on Lon Nol as a savior.

We met Lon Nol too, at military headquarters. It was all rather casual, with little sense of security. We sat in chairs—this time without drinks—around Lon Nol, a man with a large mouth and big, slow eyes, who seemed far more thoughtful than Thieu. He said that he had served Sihanouk for twelve years but that now he took a position for independence. He said he feared that the country's institutions would be destroyed if the communists came in. He gave each of us a big, thick, silver identification bracelet. He said we were the first American group, aside from journalists and advisors, to visit since 1963.

We visited refugee camps and walked around in a village leveled by an American air strike. We flew out one hundred miles to where they were building a sort of Maginot line out of bamboo, wood and stone. We went to Preet Leap, which was near Phnom Penh and the Mekong River, and helped dig trenches. I was interviewed there by CBS camera crews, and their film was aired on the evening news with Walter Cronkite. So there I was for some ten million people to see, including all my old school buddies, my family, and my mother's anti-war colleagues, leaning on a shovel and saying that if American students knew the truth they would be flocking to Kennedy Airport the way they did during the Hungarian revolution of 1956, demanding to fight for Cambodia's right for self-determination.

A day later we flew to Japan. Here we were to see an organization much farther along than ours. The Japanese branch of the Unified Family was large, disciplined, as tightly run as a battleship. Again we were met at the airport, this time with banners and cheers. We were put up in a private guesthouse with a staff for cleaning and cooking.

Moon had come to Japan after he had established missions in the United States and Europe, but he had found far more fertile ground here, and by 1967 he was even running candidates for political office. Osami Kuboki, president of the Japanese church, had run for mayor of Tokyo just this year. Moon seemed to be drawing his following in Japan more from the political mainstream than he did in the United States, where most of us could definitely be said to be disaffected types. Kuboki, for instance, had been secretary to Japan's major Buddhist party. This man, who was now in his mid-thirties and who was as broad as a sumo wrestler, was well born and well educated. According to the story he was fond of telling, one day while fasting he had had a great spiritual revelation. The world had stopped for him—all motion, all time, everything, except the sky—which swirled and boiled above him. Out of this sky came a voice which said, in effect: "This is it, the real thing." Even then, Kuboki had waited. He mortified himself for six months, collecting and selling garbage to scrape a living, and sleeping out in the open. Only then was he sure his calling was right and that he was worthy of it.

Japan was a politically fragmented country. Its coalition of communist groups was powerfully organized, and we would see them at their most effective before the visit was over. Moon, moreover, was drawing converts from both extremes of the political spectrum. This became obvious to us because the Japanese church had an odd quirk: having apparently ripped a page from the fundamentalists' Bible, they were keen on giving testimony. How happy they were—right down to the cleaning staff—to march forward and then for two hours in parade-ground voices (sometimes in their own stilted English and sometimes translated by Miss Kim or someone else) recite how they had come to the church, how many fasts they had had, all about their dreams and visions. One told us how he used to be a communist and had made bombs in a factory, but now had come to God and Moon and was working for peace. Another told how he lost half his stomach and gained his spiritual eye and could now tell when people lied. And yet another told us how he used to be an emperor-worshipping right-winger and now had come—perhaps by only the slightest flick of his political compass needle—to worship Moon.

It was through this witnessing process that we could understand how deeply appealing Moon was to Japan's reactionaries. What better way to tell it than through Arima Katayama, one of Kuboki's close connections. Katayama, now in his seventies, was a World War II fanatic, an architect of the kamikaze program who had had a role in the Hitler-Tojo pact, and a war criminal who had done time; he was now the unofficial head of Japan's right wing. It would be wrong to say he was a follower of Moon, but he clearly admired the devoted corps which Moon had raised. In his peculiar way, Katayama considered himself Moon's friend. This militant old Japanese, who looked as if he could unsheathe his samurai sword, cut you in five pieces and then resheathe his blade, all in two seconds, put it his own way: "I am Moon's dog," he told a group of Moon's followers. I was coming to understand to what a strange extent subservience was a part of the fierce Japanese character.

Katayama headed a number of big corporations, including one that might well be the world's biggest shipbuilder. As for his own religion, he seemed to have invented it, and it wasn't as crazy as it sounded when you realized that what he said brought him very close to the first Greek monist, the pre-Socratic who is generally considered to be the great-great-grandfather of modern science, Thales, who said that everything was water. Katayama carried a bilingual card that explained on the back his personal religion of "waterology." It said that water was strong, water takes all shapes, water penetrates everything, destroys silently, is eternally moving, changing, and so on.

The Japanese are a highly complicated people with a great sense of dignity and honor, and Moon seemed to understand them well. This was not so difficult to comprehend when you realized that Japanese was the only foreign language Moon spoke fluently. Moreover, he had been schooled in Japan—in engineering—and Korea, until 1945, had been occupied by the Japanese, whose culture had been well absorbed.

Right-wingers like Katayama loved Moon because he wanted Japan to rearm. After I took the two-and-half-hour supertrain ride north to Kyoto to the WACL conference, I had no difficulty in understanding how pleasantly Moon's teachings struck right-wingers in Asia. Nor was the conference limited to Asian right-wingers: Senator Strom Thurmond was the keynote speaker at the rally following this fifty-three-nation parley, which was held in a great modern conference center that looked, with all its turrets and towers, like an aircraft carrier stranded on dry ground. Anita Castro also spoke, reviling her brother as a murdering criminal about as passionately as he used to revile the capitalists in his speeches.

Kuboki was the host at the conference, which was in turn sponsored by the International Federation for Victory over Communism, in other words by Moon. In all, the conference must have cost an astronomical amount of money, perhaps three or four million dollars, and most of the money came from the fund-raising efforts of the Japanese members, largely through the street sales of flowers. (Such fundraising had not yet begun in the United States.) However, Moon's connection with the conference was far from explicit. In fact, his only obvious link was in the widely displayed poster picture of Kuboki walking with his teacher, who was not named, but who was unmistakably, to those of us who knew him, Sun Myung Moon.

Those under age twenty-five met as a conference subgroup, and I was the United States' representative. For three days we read papers, gave talks, filed reports and suggestions, acted out stratagems and counterstratagems—the main one against some Indian representatives who seemed to want to sabotage the conference through parliamentary means, using questions, motions, and delays—and ended at some posture on where the communists were and what needed to be done about them.

Kuboki was to give his closing speech in English, which would be difficult, since he didn't speak it. I wrote his speech and taught it to him by rote in a couple of hours. It was only about three hundred fifty words, and it went perfectly, except that he never, no matter how many times I drilled him, could pronounce *miracle*. So everyone left the conference expecting no milacres—whatever they were.

Kuboki and I got along nicely, speaking as well as we could through an interpreter, usually Miss Kim, who had arrived for the conference and who went on with us to Korea. (Marshall, having finished all the AYJP business and not being a member of the church, had retruned to the United States to set up a press conference which we would give jointly in early October.) Kuboki told me that President Park was one of the sponsors of the conference. He also told me that Moon was in some fear of the Park regime and there was even talk that he was marked for assassination, for religious oppression was the order of the day in the new South Korea. One of the main aims of this conference, said Kuboki, was to reassure Park that his aims and Moon's coincided.

I could hardly doubt that Moon's strategy had succeeded perfectly. His political aims were perfectly enmeshed in his religious goals, since the final cataclysm was to come in the form of World War III. They would be absolutely palatable, when they were more widely understood, to Park or Strom Thurmond or for that matter to the Nationalist Chinese. To Moon, Korea was the third Israel—modern Israel being the second after the historical first one—and it was to be reunited either under Satan, meaning always the communists, or under God, meaning the "democratic" nations. Moon strongly favored a bloc, made up of South Korea, Japan and Nationalist China, which would be powerful enough to stop Red China.

Things had gone well indeed, and well enough for Kuboki to say that we would do this again, only next time it would be in Washington in 1973. (It didn't happen, but there is no doubt that the WACL conference in Japan gave Moon the courage and inspiration for the Madison Square Garden rally of 1976.)

We returned to Tokyo briefly, where we joined in a great anticommunist rally at the Budokahn sports palace. We went out into the streets and made speeches from bus tops, and here we glimpsed how tightly organized the Japanese communists were. They came after us in the streets wearing shields and helmets and carrying kindo sticks, joining hands in a great chanting snake that undulated around us. We developed the tactic of putting our women in an outer circle around us, and it worked perfectly. They couldn't attack the women or they would get bad press. And who knows what notions of ancient chivalry they would have been violating in striking women, for the kindo sticks were related to the old ways, being a practice device for the samurai sword. How well I knew that, since the guesthouse was near a building where the sport of kindo fencing was practiced, and I can remember trying to sleep one exhausted afternoon while the crack of the sticks went on and on for hours, interrupted from time to time by great roars of applause as someone placed a particularly deft stroke.

In late September we flew on to Korea. We landed in Seoul, a booming skyscraper city of six million, full of plenty of soldiers and a great many second-class buses full of workers. From there we drove two and a half hours out to Moon's training center. This was also where Moon had his air-rifle factory, as well as a plant producing steel rods. The steel rods were apparently put to industrial uses. The air guns were, as we would see, models of a military rifle—in effect, a trainer. Moon also owned a shotgun factory, which was elsewhere in Korea. This gun was marketed commercially under the name of Tong-Il, which means unification in Korean. Elsa Reiner had told me that when Moon had come to the United States in 1969 he had proposed marketing this gun from door to door. She had been one of those who had protested vigorously. Moon had been furious at first, had taken their resistance as a kind of betrayal. But at last he had come to understand that even in gun-loving America, the door-to-door marketing of a shotgun by a religious sect would have been regarded as peculiar by some and sinister by others.

We were greeted by Young Whi Kim, who headed the Korean church. He had an engineering degree from Berkeley and holes in his pants. We would often be reminded of what a poor country Korea was. Kim was a quiet, gracious fellow in his mid-thirties who had joined Moon very early, sometime after he had gotten his engineering degree in the mid-fifties.

We were put up in a sort of barrack facility. It was newly finished and more of these dormitories were being built. Ultimately they would be used to house the factory workers. They were just installing the bathrooms, with toilets and bathtubs. I had the feeling that they were replacing a very primitive arrangement, like a hole in the ground. We had two cooks, a teenage girl and a woman in her forties, and we were served simple but good meals. We often called for *kimchi,* the Korean pickled cabbage we had learned to love from Miss Kim's cooking, and this delighted and amused our cooks. With our meals, which we ate with chopsticks, we learned to drink cold barley water. It was a healthy diet.

At about eleven, the morning after our arrival, Miles Taylor, Bennie Sutherland, Elizabeth, Cecil Meecham and I were waiting to see Moon. Except for Cecil, who had met him in the United States in 1969, it would be our first sight of the man we had come to believe was the second messiah. The experience would bring out something different in each of us.

Already Elizabeth seemed to have turned into a Japanese female, swishing around, all bows and curtsies. Miles wanted very much to be liked and loved and was very fearful that he would not be appreciated. He also grew anxious about protocol.

"Who do you think should meet him first?" Miles asked. "Don't you suppose it should be the person of the highest rank?"

"And who would that be?" asked Bennie. He had shaped up well since I had known him in Berkeley, when there was still a lot of rock music and leftover acid coursing through his veins. Now all that had been refined.

"Me," answered Miles. "I've been a follower the longest."

"Not longer than Elizabeth," chimed in Cecil.

"Oh . . . well . . . yes . . . but . . ." We all knew what Miles wanted to say but couldn't make explicit. Elizabeth was only a girl, and besides she was a crushed thing, just coming back. She didn't count for much.

"I say it's Allen," said Elizabeth, who also perfectly understood what Miles was trying to express and who probably wanted to thwart him for bringing it up. And, of course, she favored me. "He's head of the FLF. He holds the highest rank after Kirby."

I agreed, actually. After all, I had been specially treated, singled out all during this tour. But I was in no mood to do battle with Miles, who had such a domineering personality.

"Let it be Miles," I said.

"Oh, this must be him," said Elizabeth, swishing to the window.

We saw a chauffeur-driven black limousine drive up.

By the time we had advanced across the lawn to meet him,

the Reverend Moon and his wife were out of the car and standing beside it. I studied this man carefully. Like any fan meeting his favorite movie star, my first instinct was to compare him with his photograph. He seemed older. His hairline was higher and the crow's feet around his long Oriental eyes seemed more distinct. But I was not disappointed. His smile was warm. The eyes sparkled. The sense of his presence was strong. His limbs were rounded, his shoulders thick. Here he was in all three dimensions. His hand, when I clasped it in a handshake, was strong, like a laborer's. Here was a man who had done humble physical work. In one ear, I noted, was a plug of bright red wax. I'm not sure why, but I found this sign of physical imperfection endearing.

Beside him was his wife, Hak Ja Han, pretty, smiling, self-effacing, dressed as she nearly always was, in Oriental costume. Moon had on a white shirt and slacks, like a man who had been wearing a suit and had discarded his tie and jacket. Bennie particularly was fascinated with Hak Ja Han. He would tell us, weepily, how he felt he had a sort of inner communication with her. He seemed to have a mother hangup. Cecil and I, by contrast, related to the strength we sensed in Moon. Here, we decided in our discussions later, was the warrior-hero who would lead the last battle. Wasnt' it wonderful, just unbelievable, that we were right here, in on it all?

This first meeting was short; already it was ending.

"Would you like to see more of me?" asked Moon. He spoke through his driver, who also interpreted.

"Oh, yes, yes," we said.

"Then I will come tonight. I will teach you."

He walked away from us and on toward one of the workers' dorms, where he had lunch. At this time there were perhaps one hundred fifty to two hundred workers housed here, and whenever Moon came into sight of any of them they all bowed low and stayed down until he left. I had the feeling he owned these workers body and soul. They worshiped him, they followed his religion and they worked for him. I had the feeling that they were paid subsistence salaries, that in effect they donated their labor to his cause.

Moon sent for me during the dessert course.

"You and I must meet privately," he said.

I was eager to oblige him, and deeply flattered. We made an appointment for the next afternoon in Seoul.

That night we all met in one of the factory conference rooms. From about eight to eleven he spoke to us, using as an interpreter Mrs. Choi, who spoke English fluently. She was one of the three "nuns" who orbited him in a strange relationship which that term only partially describes. These women were mediums, and they brought him news from the spirit world. Miss Kim said these women sometimes even chastised Moon and he in turn would strike them. These were women without husbands—nuns in that respect also. Mrs. Choi had been deserted by her husband, who, she said, had tried to kill her when she joined Moon. She had seen Moon in a vision one night and then the next day had gone to him with supersensory accuracy, finding him in downtown Seoul.

Moon talked that night about world history, especially detailing his ideas for America, which he told us now occupied in God's world the position that Rome had held in biblical times. As I watched Moon I felt the absolute conviction that he was the messiah. Why should the messiah not be born in a poor country like Korea, which was after all the new Israel? It all made perfect sense. I felt that I was part of a young, growing movement and that we were the soul of righteousness, the hope of the world. I was gratified that I had been cast in a fairly major role. I felt specially favored to have risen in the movement so quickly.

During the three hours that Moon talked to us that night, he nibbled at two giant persimmons, which he had peeled, and sipped at a glass of barley water, which remained three-quarters full. When he left, in the stunned worshipful silence that followed, we took the remains of the fruit and drink and shared them around, each of us taking an equal share. It was a sort of spontaneous Mass.

The next afternoon I went to Moon's apartment in a run-down part of Seoul. He lived in rooms above the headquarters, where we would hold services on Sunday mornings. I saw the room where he slept alone. There was a bed, fluffed and neat, a desk and a chair, and a small window. There were flowers on the desk and calligraphy framed on the wall. We had lunch sitting cross-legged on the floor around a black lacquer table, inlaid with two swirling dragons. I had come with Mr. Kim, head of the Korean party, and at the table we joined Moon, his wife, and Mrs. Choi, who translated.

"Did you see the communists in Japan?" Moon asked me, smiling. We had finished the meal, during which our conversation had consisted of polite pleasantries.

I nodded.

"You saw how well organized they were. We are really the only group opposing them. We are the only ones with an ideology. The West is money only. In the West people will not sacrifice their lives. Are you ready to sacrifice your life?"

I nodded again. I was ready for this. More and more there was this kind of talk. We were told we must be ready to fight, to go to the front, women first. It was a sort of variation of our tactic of surrounding ourselves with our women back in Tokyo.

Moreover, being pro-war and anticommunist did not mean that Moon wanted me to give up my draft deferment and go over to Vietnam in the United States army. I had better things to do. Everyone who could get a deferment of any kind, including a C.O. status on the basis of religion, was encouraged to do so.

"We must unify and work hard. We must gain converts," Moon went on through the interpreter. "But there is so little time. Already Korea may be lost. I hope not, but it is possible."

"What do you wish me to do, Father?"

"We need support on university campuses. We must unify

the students, the faculty, and bring them with us. The faculties hold the reins of certification to all professions. If we make gains there we can shape the thinking of all America. We must win friends, we must win their trust. We must do this by serving them. We must serve them until heaven gives them to us. Do you understand?"

I did. It was part of the dogma and not to understand would mean I had not grasped his teachings. Our relationship to others, to nonbelievers, was like the relationship of Abel to Cain. Our job was to subdue Cain, to bring him to us by any means, and serving him was one of the best. It was a subtle paradox, appealing no doubt to the Oriental mind: you could dominate people by subordinating yourself to them. In the end, when they owed you everything, you literally owned them. This was in essence what Moon was doing to President Park in holding the WACL conference.

Moon's oldest son, who was nine, swept into the room. He leaped into his father's lap with complete abandon, and he encountered no reproof at interrupting us. His father laughed and jostled him. The boy carried a tablet and a pencil. As we looked on benevolently he drew for us tanks, submarines, rockets, anti-aircraft guns, all the implements of war, and all the while his father nodded approvingly.

Hyo Gin was Moon's first child by this third wife, which was what Hak Ja Han was. You were not told about previous wives when you first joined, but gradually you learned these things not with the sense that you were uncovering lies, but rather that you were peeling off layers to a deeper reality, to the heart of the artichoke. I had found out a year or so ago, from Miss Kim, that Hak Ja Han was Moon's second wife. But in Korea we found other sources of knowledge about Moon than Miss Kim, who had been our only direct link. We had even met Won Wol Kim, Moon's first disciple, in effect the first Cain of a new historical cycle. All that remained for Won Wol Kim to do was not to betray or turn against Moon, or lose his faith.

If he did not do any of these things, history could move forward.

Here, through speaking with these Korean followers, both early and late, through mediums like Mrs. Choi, and through Moon himself, we learned the story of his life. Each night, for the rest of our stay in Korea, he came to us and taught for three hours.

At this time Moon was about fifty years old. He had gone to school in Japan. When Moon was sixteen Jesus appeared to him on a mountaintop on Easter morning. Jesus told Moon that he had a mission, that his life was not his own, but belonged to God. Later, in Japan, during his studies in electrical engineering, Moon discovered, through reason and intuition, that sex was the original sin. At this time he went into the spirit world, for he was capable of that, and confronted Jesus and his disciples with this truth. Twice they denied that sex was the original sin. But the third time Moon asked, the booming voice of God was heard. He said to Moon: "You are right, and you are my son."

Moon then spent a long time, nine years, meditating and praying. He cried until his face was bloated and his eyes were swollen shut. He cried until the tears formed a puddle on his table and dripped onto the floor below and ran through the floorboards and then dripped into the room below. At this time he did no witnessing, no teaching, but many people had dreams about him and saw him in visions.

In these early years, when he returned to Korea, Moon lived with humble people, social rejects, prostitutes. There were many early betrayals. He was in Korea in 1945, when the Communist infiltrations came. In 1947 and '48 he was in the north, teaching. He had gathered a small group about him, some thirty or forty. The authorities brought him in and told him to stop his work. He didn't and they brought him in again. They beat him and tortured him, blowing out his intestines with water. Then they threw him out to die.

But he didn't die. His followers nursed him back to health,

and he resumed his teaching. The next time the authorities took him in and put him in prison camp at Hung-nam. His number was 596, which in Korean is pronounced oh-gu-rak, which is a kind of pun, because oh-gu-rak also means *innocent*. Everyone in the prison recognized him, because they were having dreams of him. They saw him sitting high on a throne. He gave away half his food each day, and yet he never lost weight. This amazed his guards, who began to realize he was a specially favored man. He worked with the rest in a mine sixteen or seventeen hours a day, but always he had time to wash his face and hands and to pray to God.

When the United States began bombing and the prison camp came under attack, the bombs never fell near Moon. The others saw that he lived a charmed life and everyone followed him around, so they would not be hit by bombs. In the end, though, the bombs destroyed the camp and he escaped the day before he was scheduled to be executed. Taking with him a friend with a broken leg, although they had only a bicycle to transport the two of them, Moon traveled six hundred miles to Pusan.

In 1960 Moon became the Lord of the Spirit World. As such he ruled all creatures of that world, including the spirits of all people dead and unborn and all other spirits, both evil and good. In that all-important year he was married to his present wife and his true mission began. It is to be finished in the year 1981, after three cycles of seven, when the holocaust is to come. Only those sealed by the messiah will survive.

Moon had had two previous wives, but they had turned against him. One, however, had come back to the fold, we were told, but no longer as his wife. She was now merely a faithful follower. In 1969 Moon's thirteen-year-old son by one of these women was killed, decapitated when he put his head out of a speeding train. This boy died because the Korean church was not faithful enough. Mrs. Choi and the other mediums saw a red tide pouring into Korea. It was a sign that the communists were again about to try to take over all of

Korea. Moon called for everyone to work. He called three
times, but they did not help him. After the third call, he picked
up a stone and put it in the gap in the wall—the demilitarized
zone—through which the red tide was pouring. That stone was
the life of his son, sacrificed for the sake of South Korea.

There was yet another son of Moon's by a previous wife.
This was Saejun, who was born in 1946. I met him there in
Korea in 1970, when he was twenty-four. Moon now has seven
children by Hak Ja Han.

We were to understand that Moon's mission was conditional, as Christ's mission had been conditional. Christ had
not been meant to fail, according to Moon's teaching. Christ
had failed because he had been betrayed and, like Christ,
Moon, too, could be betrayed. He was now in a process of bar-
gaining with God. If he could gain such and such number of
converts in one hundred twenty countries, then God would
grant him more power. Moon called himself the Lord of the
Second Advent now, but as to whether he would be fulfilled
as the messiah would depend on the response and work of his
followers. Consequently our first priority was in gaining converts. We were also to remain absolutely obedient to Moon.

We were told that if you lied to Moon directly concerning
his mission, his voice could kill you.

One afternoon Kim took me to a restaurant where we sat
cross-legged on the floor and cooked our own meat—thin
marinated strips of beef—on a fire built inside a sort of in-
verted colander. This was called *pulgoggi* and it was delicious.

Kim then took me to a Korean herbalist who, I was told,
also had a medical degree from an American university, but
preferred Oriental remedies. This fellow had only to put three
fingers on my arm to tell me that my energy was running the
wrong way and that I was eating far too much salt. He gave me
a prescription for a potion, which we got filled. As far as I
could tell this concoction had ginseng, turtle shell, herbs and

roots and other ground up dried things which I probably wouldn't care to know about—toads, beatles, lizards, buffalo horn, squirrel gonads, and so on. We took the stuff and boiled it up for an hour, as instructed. When it was cool enough, I drank it down, and I found myself immediately invigorated.

Another afternoon Hak Ja Han took us in to Seoul to buy clothes—for the men, suits, which were made up quickly and cleverly by batteries of tailors. These were very like the Hong Kong suits which are so famous. Hak Ja Han made a great production of holding the fabrics, most of them good British woolens, to our skins to choose the most flattering hues. I was measured for a sleek gray gabardine suit, which was ready in a matter of days. I had the impression through all of this that Hak Ja Han also understood more English than she let on. I was beginning to suspect that this kind of pretense was common among Orientals. I thought it was as much as anything engendered by the Orientals' great sense of dignity—face, as it is often called—and accordingly I did not find the trait particularly sinister.

It was fall now in the Korean mountains, though the sun was still hot during the day. In the cool evenings we gathered together, though whether it was a meeting, a service or a training session or all three, I couldn't really say. As in our Sunday morning services, there would be sermons and prayers. Nearly all our functions began and ended with prayers. As in the training sessions, there were tirades against Satan and the communists that would have satisfied any fundamentalist This was a living religion, and in the near future—within our lifetimes —real people were going to roast in a real hell, albeit a hell of napalm and nukes as well as natural disasters, and then the Kingdom of Heaven would be established on earth. This was nothing like the namby-pamby Protestant congregations led by watery-blooded ministers who would have choked on the thought of anyone sitting out there really going to hell. And where hell wasn't really possible, neither was heaven.

Mr. Ishi would stand up and tell about how the Reds were gaining control of his native Japan. Then he would sing a Korean folk song, perhaps "Toragi," a common one. The Korean members loved to hear a Japanese sing a Korean folk song because the older ones could remember when the Japanese ruled them and when their own songs, not to mention their own language, were held in utter contempt by their occupiers.

Ever since Kirby Smith had arrived with his bride-to-be, Julie, I had been in trouble. No doubt Kirby now saw me, just as he had seen other strong personalities, such as Neil Salonen and Elsa, as a threat to his leadership. I had been getting a great deal of attention and Kirby didn't like it. No one could really fault me on the performance of my job, though, unless, like Becky, who was also a bride-to-be, Salonen's, they were going to attack me for being riddled with Pride. However, my detractors found a much better weapon to use against me: Elizabeth Burns. Our flirting had been noticed, and the worst construction had been put on it. It seems that after her previous fall, Elizabeth would never again be above suspicion. She was like an ex-con the police hauled in to grill after every crime in her neighborhood. It was as if no one could believe a girl with such obvious sexual attractiveness and vitality could ever be above sexual temptation. To them she was the archetypal Eve.

I saw that in hanging around with her I was gaining a reputation for being sex-obsessed. Finally I went to Elizabeth and told her that although I liked her and maybe even loved her, I was now going to stay away from her altogether and furthermore was going to harden my heart against her. Unless I was going to marry her, which I wasn't, there was simply no place in the organization even for chaste affection between the sexes.

We were finding out, in fact, that there was to be no condoned pre-nuptial rite, no courtship in the Unified Family at all. On October 21, Moon married seven hundred young couples. Ten couples, including Kirby and Julie and Neil and Becky, had arrived from the United States for the ceremony, and others had come from France, Germany, Holland, Italy, England and Austria. But the Japanese and the Koreans were simply presenting themselves en masse: they did not arrive as couples. Moon chose their mates for them, and in just a few hours he matched them up and married them to someone they had most likely not even known the day before. While it was true that the American and European couples had chosen each other, already we could feel pressure to do it the Japanese and Korean way: to marry by lottery, in effect.

Such a method would, of course, keep the great demon of sex in even greater check and serve as well to increase Moon's dominion over his group. Marriage was his most important sacrament. Our supreme earthly goal was to marry and fructify, building a larger and larger family under God. At first Moon had married small groups—but always groups—and they were to grow larger and larger as his earthly power grew, preferably by geometric leaps and bounds. He had married thirteen couples in the United States in 1969—Frank and Elise being the first of them—and they were to represent the thirteen original colonies. Numbers were significant to Moon, who always showed a cabalistic attitude toward figures. By this time he should have been marrying one hundred sixty-nine American couples, thirteen times thirteen, a geometric progression, instead of ten, but of course we knew something had gone wrong with Frank and Elise. Fortunately the Oriental church was doing fine, and we were here to see and learn and eventually to emulate it.

With everyone tsk-tsking me over Elizabeth, I was not unhappy when I saw a means of escape. Marshall Miller sent me a telegram asking if I could come back to give a joint press conference with him on October 6. I went with this to Moon, and he said: "Clearly you have responsibilities elsewhere; you must go." The next day Mrs. Choi and Won Wol Kim, the original disciple, took me to the airport.

"He trusts you," said Kim through Mrs. Choi. "Can you serve him as I have?"

I blinked and looked at him a moment.

"Yes," I said.

A strange thing happened to me during my layover in Tokyo. I did not get in touch with any members of the Unified Family. Instead I stayed the night in a cheap airport hotel, sharing a room with two American sailors. When they sent for massage girls, I sent for one, too. The girls, clad in bikinis, came to our room, oiled us up and rubbed us down. They were not prostitutes, but by the time they finished I was almost crazed. I was going out to get a whore in Tokyo. I had about two hundred dollars in pocket money left from the four hundred I had come overseas with, some of it from my parents and some from my AYJP salary. I scrabbled through my luggage looking for the traveler's checks. They were gone! I looked again. And again. No checks. By now I was breathing hard. The sweat was pouring down my face, soaking my clothes.

The next day, suspended over the clouds in a jet airliner somewhere over the Pacific Ocean, I was glad I had lost the money. Satan had tried to snatch me, and he had almost succeeded. I had come fresh from the presence of the Master, his touch still glistening on my shoulder, and I had almost fallen.

This strange battle was entirely within my own mind, of course. When I arrived in Washington and checked my luggage I immediately found the checks, more or less where they ought to be. I had simply deceived myself. My mind had been divided against itself. I did know, however, that had I gone to a whore that night in Tokyo, I would have been out of the Unified Family forever, from that moment.

That was one part of my mind—concealed from me, dark, inchoate, a sea monster that had momentarily broken the surface and then resubmerged. As for the other part, the conscious part with which I lived day to day, it told me that I was overwhelmed with Sun Myung Moon. I was very impressed with the energy of the Japanese branch, with the poverty and devotion of the Koreans, with the daily sacrifice of them all—to a degree that we in the United States never approached—and I told myself that I felt a renewed sense of commitment and purpose.

I arrived in Washington on the morning of the press conference. I was met at the airport by Sharon Panikkar, the wife of a Hindu who had joined us recently. She drove me straight to the hotel where Marshall had set up the press conference. It was well attended and well along when I arrived. We told about our tour through Vietnam and Cambodia. We said that Nixon's Vietnamization was working. It was a variation of our Saigon conference. I don't think we got much play in the news from this press conference either. The media would have gobbled the stuff up in '67—when *The New York Times* was printing government press releases practically verbatim—but now, three years later, the tide had clearly turned against the war. At any rate, I wasn't surprised. I had no illusions about the press being unbiased.

I went back to work for the American Youth for a Just Peace with Marshall, speaking in the evenings at Lions Clubs, Rotarian functions, once to a black Jaycees group. My speech was basic anticommunist stuff, full of facts and figures drawn from USIA pamphlets as well as my own new observations abroad, proving that the Reds were worse than the Nazis.

On Upshur Street we found a new boy on the block: Willard Zeigler, a thirty-eight-year-old chiropractor. He was snuggling into Miss Kim's vacant bed—with her permission—with his wife. Zeigler was a hard-line macho type, and he had been rather terrorizing the rank and file while the leadership, including Miss Kim, was away. He was a short vigorous fel-

low—rather Oriental looking except for his ruddy complexion
—of German descent and from Queens. He had previously
been a chauffeur for a medium who was traveling around the
country trying to hook up one hundred forty-three other mediums—here it was again, the significance of numbers—so all
one hundred forty-four of them, twelve by twelve, could wait
for the messiah. Zeigler had decided that the mediums were
off on a wrong tangent: the messiah was already here. Willard
had joined up.

Zeigler was a strong personality, and in our situation, where
there was no orderly process for assuming leadership—in fact
another person supposedly had been left in official charge—the
most powerful tended to take over. Despite our pretensions
otherwise, we lived in nothing much better than a primitive
dog pack and there was constant testing of leaders and jockeying for position. Moreover, there was a pecking order as rigid
as that in any barnyard. You could immediately sense where
you stood at a given moment, though your position was constantly changing. At times a certain stability would be established, though nothing really long-lasting, but now all that was
shattered because the leadership was still abroad. Except for
me, of course, but I was an organization man, unproven as a
leader of people.

When Cecil Meecham came home a few days after me, he
and I and Mona gathered into a coterie that effectively held
Zeigler and his supporters at bay. Mona was a powerful ally,
because with her mind-reading powers she was much feared
and she could dominate any meeting. Very likely this was
why she had been shunted off into the peculiar satellite orbit
she occupied around us.

This worked until the others returned from Korea, but then
it seemed that we could not regain our original balance. For
one thing, our two ranking couples, Kirby and Julie and Neil
and Becky, seemed utterly stunned to find themselves married.
No doubt Kirby, never a particularly exhortative or secure
leader, found much of his energy drawn inward. Then a

recent recruit, and a married one at that, David Stevens, accused Cecil and me of having a sex triangle with three-hundred-pound Mona. This was no doubt based on his own receptivity to vibes, things he had overheard and seen, including Mona's hugging and ass-patting, which had previously passed as her special privilege, and the workings of his own intellect, which was pure paranoia, though no one there used such words and I could certainly not have drawn upon such a psychological term to defend myself.

Furthermore, this charge, totally cooked up out of his own fears and repressions, was believed. I was, after the trouble with Elizabeth, practically a certified sex pervert. There was no gathering of evidence, no interviewing of witnesses, no trial. We were guilty because everyone thought we were, and we were in disgrace. This served several purposes. The upstart Allen, disliked by many, possibly feared by Kirby, was deposed from the FLF office. This was convenient for Neil Salonen, who was now back in Kirby's good graces, no longer a threat but a staunch ally, very likely through the sharing of the new strains of marriage. He would resume control of the political arm of the church; he would not return to Colorado. And Mona, that giant enfant terrible, still resented by Kirby for foreseeing and telling me of my FLF appointment, was pushed into an orbit farther out. In the light of these developments, I might well wonder now whether Elizabeth's supposed previous sexual transgression had ever happened. Her only sin might well have been her bad fortune, in these ranks at least, of being extremely pretty.

So my FLF days were over. There would be no more cloak and dagger, no more weenie-roasting in the upstate New York sunset with Marshall Miller, no more lunches with professors. Technically I resigned my office, though in fact I was deposed by an oligarchical fiat, which was simply the way things were done in the Unified Family.

Being in disgrace was not all that bad, I found out. As soon as you fell, everyone started forgiving you. I played Cain to their Abel. That was the dogma. Their job was to subdue me with their love and take one tiny step toward reversing the course of history, in which so far Cain had nearly always subdued Abel with his hatred. Love was seen as a powerful, dominating force. The weak were loved, the strong dispensed love. Love flowed downward, not upward, not really even back and forth, though Moon's philosophy did incorporate the notion of a universal duality and polarity, of a constant give and take, the Oriental yin and yang.

It was a Humpty-Dumpty world, and all you did when you got shattered was to start putting yourself together again. Sometimes it did not even take too long. Neil Salonen was rehabilitated now. And even Frank and Elise were back from Boston, where they had set up a center and a home-cleaning business. Frank had pulled it all together and was well on the way to multiplying. He had gotten Elise pregnant.

Although I was still somewhat resentful at being forgiven for something I had never done, it was certainly better than not being forgiven. I conquered my rancor and set about being a dutiful soldier in the ranks. An inevitable hiatus followed our travels, our meeting with Moon, the marriages. We knew we had to make money and get converts, but we weren't sure how.

We put on a charity drive for a reformatory, canvassing door-to-door for contributions and books. Our help was welcome. At this time we had had no bad publicity. In fact, people scarcely knew who we were. Most people had never heard of Moon. We seemed to be just another clean-cut religious group. We had even been cleared by the Nixon government, I discovered when I solicited my uncle in Tennessee, who was president of a bank. (We were encouraged to press our family and relatives for contributions.) Uncle Jim, who had very high local standing and good connections, went straight to the FBI, no doubt because his sister-in-law, my mother, had told him I was working for some right-wing front. But the FBI gave us an A-1 patriotic rating. It was hard to get on the wrong side of the FBI if you were against communism.

Little did they know. We collected a good many books and something over $5,000. We turned in all the books and a small fraction of the money. We simply kept most of the money. It was okay for Abel to lie to Cain, though the parable that best illustrated our morality was that of Jacob, who stole Esau's birthright. Moon's system was simply one of the many in which the end justifies the means. Lying and stealing were okay as long as you were doing it for the sake of good.

The reformatory episode turned a couple of people's stomachs. In a sense participating in it was probably a kind of test, just as teenage gang initiates must do some awful deed to seal their bond with the rest. At any rate, we did not repeat this particular sleight-of-hand.

Instead we turned our energy to getting recruits and holding them. To this end it was decided that we, as national headquarters in the nation's capital, would set up a training program. Moon had let us know in no uncertain terms that we had failed him in recruiting. While he was claiming hundreds of thousands of followers in Japan and Korea, we in the United States numbered only two or three hundred. The messiah as yet had not even a toehold in the greatest nation, the Rome of the new historical cycle.

The program was to be called Level II. After the outlying centers around the country had brought their converts in and kept them for three months or so, insuring their hold over them, they would send them to us for a ten-day indoctrination, in batches of forty or fifty. I was to be the political lecturer, meaning I taught the last part of the *Divine Principle*. I was to give four lectures, the first being an analysis of Marxism, the second a catalogue of the results of communism, the third an analysis of North Korean Reds and a history of Korea, and the fourth about how Moon fit into it all. The message was that, politically speaking, we had the world on our shoulders.

For Level II we rented another house, on North Carolina Avenue, down behind the Capitol. The household was headed by Frank and Elise, who were in charge of showing the new converts what the ideal couple under Moon was like. It was no doubt also decided it would be good for a sex pervert like me to work under Frank, who had conquered his own sexual problems.

Elsa came along, too, having been relieved of the necessity of returning to St. Louis, where a center she had set up was moving along by itself. Elsa put together a series of lectures on Chapter II of the *Divine Principle*, the fall of man. She analyzed four or five religions and showed that in all of them sex was really the original sin. Miles took the lectures on Chapter I, the principle of creation, which was always the easiest to understand and like. He showed real flair in this project, using color slides of paintings and statues and icons through the ages, as well as classical music. His polished product even led to talk of making a *Divine Principle* movie to be shown in churches.

I found Miles every bit as overbearing as before, only now, in my reduced rank, he was psychically mauling me. Furthermore, I was sorry that Elsa, whom I liked very much, supported him in this. I was the low man for a long time, if anything lower even than Dawn Dixon.

Dawn was another California beauty, from the Los Angeles center. She had a strong, athletic body, auburn hair, lovely green eyes and a bouncy, optimistic way about her. She had a quick smile and she was disliked for it.

"Why do people have sex, Allen?" she asked one day when we were sitting alone.

"I dunno. Why do you think they do?"

"I just can't understand it. Have you ever had sex, Allen?"

"Sure."

"You have?" Her eyes widened. "I thought sex was a sin, *the* sin. Why would you have done that?"

"It was before I understood things, Dawn."

"Oh."

Dawn just oozed sex appeal and didn't want to shoulder its burdens. Now in her late twenties, she wanted to remain in a childlike state.

I also found out that Frank still had a few questions about sex, even though he had supposedly straightened out the main things.

"Do you think oral sex is okay?" he asked one day when we were alone in the car, driving on some errand.

"I think it's okay to do anything in bed with your wife, as long as you don't hurt each other." My answer came from my own father's sex lecture, many years ago. I figured it still applied to Frank.

"You know," Frank went on, "when Elise and I were up in Boston we went to a lot of blue movies."

I was rather surprised, but I didn't let on.

"I don't see anything wrong with that."

There wasn't either, not even according to the *Divine Principle*. We were expected to just know certain things. If something was frivolous, or harmful to the body, or distracting from higher duties, then it was wrong in that context. For instance, pornography would have been wrong for me, would have stoked up desires I could not satisfy. But for Frank, trying to save his marriage, it was perfectly all right. Moon set up only one prohibition, premarital sex, and if that was followed, everything else seemed to fall naturally into place. Almost never was there a discipline problem in the Unified Family.

My talks about sex with Frank—this one and others that we had later—backfired on me. It happened after Level II was finished in May, having served to indoctrinate some five batches of converts. There were simply no more recruits for the time being. We asked ourselves what was next, and the

answer was, logically, Level III, which would begin in the
fall. Level III was more of the same, only deeper, longer
and more intensive. Meanwhile the summer passed unevent-
fully for me. I went to summer school at American University.
I took four courses, two in psychology, one in anthropology
and one in African history taught by a Marxist Hindu who
gave me the top grade in the class. In fact, I got three A's and
a B that term. My grades had improved remarkably since
Sewanee.

I was on the ascent again, almost patched up, when I made
a bad slip. I hadn't been talking to Mona, but I figured all
that had blown over. When she invited me to dinner—I actually told Frank about it—I went. We had a big feed at Trader
Vic's on Sixteenth Street and got drunk on luscious rum
drinks filled with fruit and gossiped about everyone and everything. Mona was always lively and entertaining. But when I
came back something snapped in Frank. He was furious at
me. He said I was still sex-obsessed and he quoted my conversations with him, which as far as I was concerned were
initiated by him, as evidence of my unreformed character.
And the kid I was rooming with in the basement, another
troubled paranoiac, said he was having bad dreams because
of my sexual vibrations. I was condemned again.

I was demoted even further. I would not be a lecturer in
Level III. I was going back to being a student. I was aghast.
I had been expecting to be reinstated, like Frank and Salonen,
but here I was getting pushed even further down.

I went to Miss Kim. She was the power behind the power.
She was everyone's confidante; she knew all that was going
on behind the scenes. And she had always liked me, favored
me.

I remember talking to her as the late afternoon light faded
in the kitchen. She sat with her elbows on the plastic table-
cloth. Behind her on the shelves our motley, tacky collection
of dishes was stacked. In the background the refrigerator
hummed.

I told her the whole story in a great state of agitation. As I spoke she pulled the pins from her hair, which I had never seen down. Her beautiful blue-black hair cascaded about her shoulders. It was thick and long. It reached down to the middle of her back. There was great meaning in the gesture, I thought. I felt I was seeing the unveiling of a celestial being. What she said did not disappoint me.

Miss Kim had always been a critical follower of the Reverend Moon. Once she had told me that she believed he had some years ago lost his ability to read minds and travel in the astral world. That was why he had to employ the three mediums now. Once she had hinted that Moon was not the messiah, but only in the line of the messiah. He was an Abraham figure, and his son or his grandson would be the true messiah. This was utter heresy, of course, and this was in the back of my mind as Miss Kim spoke.

"Do not worry, young Allen. Frank has many problems and you must bear with him. All this will smooth out later. Meanwhile, I have powers myself. I will look after you. You are under my protection."

I left the interview completely satisfied. I felt that I had the blessing of a real-life good witch of the East. I did not know exactly what she meant, but I had faith in her. I recalled what had happened the last time I had come to her discouraged. I did become a student in Level III, and I bore with it the best I could. I was a good follower, and by November came the news that made me determined to remain one. The Reverend Moon was coming here!

In December 1971, about a week before Christmas, Moon was present for our Level III graduation, which was held at a church we rented across the street. We had been renting its basement for our Sunday services for a long time. I got a small printed certificate saying that I had graduated from Level III. Presumably I was rehabilitated.

Moon stayed in the Upshur Street house, in the "parents'

room," which was a room we kept in every center, specially furnished and waiting, should the day come for the visit of Our Leader. He lay low for about a week. He watched a lot and he conferred privately with many people. I was not one of them; I was no longer in the inner circle. Then, on the day before Christmas, he came out of his room and began to speak. And he kept on preaching all through Christmas and on to the beginning of the new year, for the greater part of seven consecutive days.

Moon talked for many hours each day, until people began to fall asleep, and he would awaken them with a shout or a shake or even a slap across the face.

He told us many things. He told us that the messiah was now in the new Rome, that as of now he had made far more progress than Jesus ever had, though he was also far short of completing his mission. But from now on, his mission was here. Moon would not perform miracles, by the way, because miracles were merely crowd pleasers, nothing serious. Jesus' miracles were a sign of failure, Moon said.

Moon retold the parables of the Bible, adding his own interpretations. Mrs. Choi, the medium, translated for him, as she continued to do when he was in the United States and speaking more or less privately, to his own followers. When he spoke publicly, as he was preparing to do, for his mission was taking outward shape, Colonel Pak was the translator.

Moon told us about the nature of sin. The main duality in God's creation was between good and evil. To do evil was to sin, but since everyone thought of themselves as good, how did we know when we were sinning? The answer was that when we were working for ourselves, we were sinning. When we were working for others, we could be sure that we were doing good. Even if we did things that seemed good to others, if we did these things out of our own vanity and egoism, then we were doing evil. Motive counted very heavily in Moon's system. Just as we could lie for good motives, and thus be doing God's work, we could tell the truth for bad motives and be doing Satan's will.

Such a psychology kept us at constant war with ourselves, and if it succeeded in its aims, our energy would be constantly projected outward. Moon's was not a religion of introspection, of mysticism, of finding a oneness with God or Nature, nor even a religion of peace or beauty. It was rather a path of action. He would tell us what to think, and our duty was to obey him. His was the perfect religion for those who wished to escape from themselves.

In those seven days Moon mapped out a plan of action and told it to us. He would begin a One World Crusade and he would speak for three days in each of seven cities. A number of us would be formed into mobile bus teams, whose job would be to go into each city as an advance guard. These people would rent the hall for him to speak, sell tickets, do publicity, preach in the streets and then, when at last the Master arrived, move on to the next city on the list and do the same thing. About all this there was an atmosphere of breathless urgency. This was not something that was to happen in the far future or even the near future, but right now. It was to begin even before the month of January was out.

But that was only part of the beginning of his mission, merely the bringing of the word. After having gotten our followers, we wanted to hold them. For that we needed more centers, at least one in every state, including Hawaii and Alaska. Despite our best efforts so far, we had centers in only eight states. We would immediately send out missionaries to all the other states.

In those seven days Moon also prayed many times, and each prayer ended with him in tears. He pulled out his big white handkerchief, snapped it open with a flourish, wiped his eyes and blew his nose. He even sang to us at times; his voice was not pretty, but it was powerful. He sounded like a wounded water buffalo. Moon's voice had great range, and sometimes, in contrast to the low ranges of his singing, it rose in passion to a mere mouse's squeak. All in all he was a gigantic, an enveloping personality.

One of the sad things that happened for those of us who knew and loved Miss Kim—and particularly for me, since I was under her protection—was that Moon deposed her, abruptly, impatiently, bitterly, though privately. He was angry; he told her she had failed. We heard that he told her she must assume in regard to him the role of a child. She must learn everything all over again.

There was great excitement in the center. Although many of the older members were upset—there were conservatives here as much as anywhere—most of the rest of us considered that something approaching an empire, complete with dukedoms and fiefs, was up for grabs. This was a whole new cast of the dice; Moon had picked up everything and rolled it over, including Miss Kim. Before the month was out Kirby was out as president, having been found too slow to dance to the new tempo. Neil Salonen, an agile mover, replaced him and kept the job as president.

Miles chose to go to the Maryland center, and Elsa was going with him. These were the personalities that had dominated me in past months, and they wanted me to come along as spiritual director. I had always imagined myself as a teacher, and though I was attracted by all the hoopla surrounding the One World Crusade, this was where I chose to go. Miles was taking over the Maryland operation from his own older brother, William, who was going out to found a center in North Dakota.

With six others we rented a split-level ranch house in a lower-middle-class neighborhood a mile and a half from the University of Maryland campus; for that was the field where we chose to battle for young souls. Each day I would go onto the campus, select a spot, for instance the steps of the library during change of classes, and begin a five-minute political harangue against communism. Sometimes I carried an amplifier, but mostly I just used my voice, which I was training. My aim, and sometimes I did succeed in it, was to draw a group around me for discussion, heated or otherwise. Often, though, I was simply ignored or looked over curiously from a cautious distance. This might have been discouraging or even crushing to an ordinary human being. To someone who believed he was carrying the word of God, it was not.

Meanwhile Miles, Elsa, and Jeffrey Collins, a brilliant sort of jack-of-all-trades and former Jehovah's Witness, were turning their minds toward fund-raising. They hit upon the idea of making and selling candles. For many days our kitchen was a jumble of molds, boxes of sand and coffee pots filled with paraffin. We made some and sold them ourselves, and we sent a batch to the New York center, where we had good connections. Normie Davis, who was from North Carolina, was able to produce masterpiece candles, including an enormous one that I recall had a yellow sun that burnt down and lit, when it had consumed itself, a silver moon.

But soon we had, for our purposes, the perfect candle. It was a brandy snifter filled with wax with a wick. It was a snap to make and easy to sell. Before long Jeffrey had gone down into the basement with an empty oil drum, several feet of copper tubing and a gas heater and had whipped up a candle factory. We could make hundreds of candles in a week. After paying for materials, paraffin, wicks and case after case of snifters, and discounting our labor, which was free, the candles cost us about forty cents apiece. We sold them on the streets for a dollar.

By April we had about tripled our membership, raising it to twenty-one. Already we had outgrown our four-bedroom house. We were looking for a big place to buy, and Jeffrey, acting on an uncanny hunch, seemed to have found it effortlessly. Jeffrey, among his many other talents, had a nose for real estate. He had once been in the Young Americans for Freedom and the Students for a Democratic Society at the same time. He was politicaly ambidextrous—right and left at once. At any rate, this place he had found looked like the House of Usher, complete with ancient curtains and Edwardian furniture. It was on a hill in Upper Marlboro, on an eleven-acre site, and it was offered for sale for $120,000.

We looked it over and decided we would take it. The house was called Oak Wood, but we learned it had originally been named Mount Ararat, after Noah's mountain. It was ordained to be ours.

The only trouble was that we needed a down payment of over $20,000. We set about raising the money. We made candles endlessly and sold them tirelessly on the streets. Some people borrowed from their parents. And by June we had $13,000—a lot of money, but not enough. We asked the national headquarters to co-sign a note with us, but Salonen refused. It seemed our hopes were dashed. Then Miss Kim advanced us, to our astonishment, $10,000. Deposed or not, she certainly did have her powers. We never did learn precisely where she got the money. In gratitude, after we bought the house, we asked her to come and live in it, but she declined.

Moon went on his speaking tour, and it was not a great success, not that anyone could realistically assess the results in the Unification Church, which we now called ourselves. The family had grown into a full-fledged religious movement. As yet no one applied the term "Moonie" to us. Moon did not, of course, announce to auditoriums full of strangers that he was the messiah. That always came later. Rather he played the role of his own John the Baptist: Christianity was in crisis and the last days were around the corner, so you'd better get ready. Moon's preaching wasn't so different from many a fundamentalist crusader's, and no doubt many among his audiences found him curiously familiar. Perhaps the main difference was that he didn't speak English, but even his method of preaching through his interpreter, Colonel Pak, left its particular impression.

"To you, I am dumb," he told his audience. "And to me, you are deaf," he would go on, explaining that he could manifest himself only through the medium of interpretation. Thus he was more shrouded in mystery and, in a sense, more in control. Colonel Pak seemed like a puppet or a ventriloquist's dummy into which Moon breathed life.

Meanwhile, we moved into Upper Marlboro, and Jeffrey rebuilt the candle factory down in the big crumbly old basement. Our production easily moved into thousands of candles per day, if we worked in shifts. We sold the candles ourselves and made them for centers in other states to peddle. We would sell them to the other centers at cost, not counting labor. We quickly became a most prosperous center, not only in fund-raising, but in gaining members as well. We developed an appealing way of recruiting, giving dinners and dances and showing movies. With our wonderful house and our warmth, we gained more and more members and stimulated lots of interest. At our peak we had nearly forty adults living with us, as well as some eight children and tots.

I hung out a lot at the University of Maryland, where I was also taking a couple of courses, including one literary criticism course with a professor who had known my grandfather. At an ecumenical meeting I met one of the campus chaplains, Michael Gates, a Methodist, who was to be our first big success in domination-through-submission.

Gates was in his mid-thirties, balding and bespectacled; he had a pretty, upwardly mobile wife and a spoiled five-year-old daughter—a real terror when the Gateses came to dinner, as they often did. We pretended to be absolutely taken with Gates. Often I would bring our whole membership to his Sunday sermons, which had never been so well attended. I told the girls, particularly, to sit up front, seek eye contact and nod a lot. Sometimes we even printed and distributed leaflets advertising his sermons.

Gates decided we were extremely smart and had good taste. He knew we had some kind of theology of our own, but he never bothered to find out about it. As our reward, he would come out to Upper Marlboro and lecture us on the Old Testament. As he was a seminary graduate, Gates was well read in philosophy and theology, and we learned a great deal from him. The main use we had for him and for the others on whom we used this approach was to seem more integrated, more broadly based, less radical, generally more palatable than in fact we were. In a word, we used Gates as a front. We tried to snatch whatever souls we could in the murky waters between him and ourselves.

Our relationship with Gates was hypocritical at least, dishonest at most. Our morality permitted and encouraged it. With him and others, we formed friendships that weren't really friendships. We laughed and talked with Gates when he came to dinner, and with his wife and child as well. We spoke a great deal about love and good and the Kingdom of Heaven, but the fact was that we loved very little. Even among ourselves, our lives seemed to break down into this endemic, constant intriguing and jockeying for advantage.

Jeffrey had been in the YAF and SDS at the same time, and I had flipped from peacenik to warhawk without a blink. Suzie Shelton had been in the Progressive Labor Party and heaved bricks at cops in riots and had been ready to go to Cuba and cut sugarcane for Castro, and now she was with Moon and just as rabidly anticommunist. (This stormy-tempered, plump blonde still spoke the slang of the radical left, though.) The lives of many of the rest of us embodied less striking but nevertheless similar self-contradictions. Moon seemed to unite these disparities. He appealed to a childish antisocial ego while at the same time seeming to obliterate it. It was a subtle paradox, something of a conjuring act, but in the end we broke down into the ingredients of which we were made, one of the main ones being the hungry ego.

About this time it was decided that Moon should have a place of his own, and a wonderful place at that. An appropriately grand place was found, a mansion on an estate north of New York City in Tarrytown. This estate, once owned by a liquor magnate in the early part of the century, was called Belvedere; it cost $800,000. We, the American Unification Church, were going to raise the $200,000 down payment, thus beginning our first major fund-raising drive.

Meetings were held to decide how the money should be raised. Upper Marlboro backed candle sales and we offered to make the candles, but Salonen and others were in favor of raffles. So raffles were held, and through two months, July and August, very little money was raised. Then Salonen had an idea of his own: candle sales. A great crash effort was set in motion, what we called a "forty-day condition."

We worked in the candle factory around-the-clock, turning out three to four thousand candles a day. These we sent to other centers, which were working just as hard selling them in the streets all over the United States. In the end we made well over the amount for the down payment. During this time we, for our part, kept no financial records and paid no taxes, since the Unification Church was incorporated as a nonprofit, tax-exempt religious institution. Belvedere was bought.

"Heaven gave me this," a triumphant Moon said when it was bought. The statement didn't sit well with those who knew about it, but fortunately the news didn't sift down to the rank and file who had pounded the pavements selling those candles. Moon got a surge of confidence out of all this, and the Upper Marlboro branch stood very high in his estimation. It must have been clear that, heaven or not, the money would not have been raised without the candle factory.

In many ways the whole operation epitomized Moon's financial operations. The essential thing is that we donated our labor, and did it around the clock, as we later would many times again. As far as I know, the same thing was done abroad, in Japan, Korea and Europe. Monumental sums of money can be raised in such circumstances. People have been astounded at the sums Moon has had at his disposal at various times and have jumped to the conclusion that it came from outside sources, including South Korea. While I have no knowledge of money coming from any such outside sources, I have seen what a large band of fanatical devotees can do with simple street sales when there are no taxes and little or no overhead. At times drivers from other centers showed up to buy our candles with vans full of tons of coins which had been taken in through street sales. It was a concrete demonstration that every little bit adds up. I would estimate that in two years the Upper Marlboro factory brought in nearly two million dollars. Looking at us on any given day, no one would have thought us capable of more than a few thousand a year.

Some months later Moon came out to visit us at Upper Marlboro. It was a gesture of appreciation. He walked all over the grounds and gave us advice on how to take care of the trees. He saw the candle factory, asked questions, and nodded approvingly. Candles were now well established as a major source for fund-raising.

On the grounds Moon spotted a couple of our new young men wearing long hair. He called us together.

"I have a favor to ask you," he said in a low voice. Sometimes he spoke halting English without an interpreter. "I want to ask you to cut your hair. I won't tell you to do it, but I will ask you."

The next day they had the bank-clerk haircuts we all wore. There was simply no discipline problem in the Unification Church. Converts quickly came to understand that even if they did believe Moon was the messiah and wanted to work for him, there was no room for them unless they understood the *Divine Principle*. And once they understood, it was the source of their very identity.

After Moon arrived in this country, a more rigid dress code was instituted. While we had never been particularly sloppy, now a closer watch was kept on the length of our hair. And in public we wore, almost invariably, conservative suits, with white shirts and ties—what Moon himself wore. While the rest of the country's youth were getting "greened" and slipping into comfortable faded denims, the garb of Consciousness III, we were dressing totally for the eyes of others. We dressed without regard for our own comfort or style, and the result was a strange but unmistakable style of our own. What came through, I believe, is the denial of self, what some people would call the "zombie" look.

The visit went well. Moon was pleased. We were gaining membership. The layout was attractive. He was ready to leave when Miles reminded him: "Master, you have not seen the parents' room."

Moon and his entourage followed us to the upstairs room which we had furnished with a fine Oriental rug, silver candlesticks, a fireplace with brass andirons, bureaus, chairs, a couch, and to top off this perfectly appointed chamber, a big, framed color blowup of Mr. and Mrs. Moon.

Moon broke into delighted laughter. He kicked off his shoes and sat on the couch. With his slitted eyes, the accentuated crow's feet, the wide mouth in the flat, round face, he seemed to have more than one smile going at once. He called for the whole group to sit around him, and he looked at us with new eyes.

"You are a success," he said to Miles. "You are doing good work."

Elsa, Jeffrey, and I beamed. Although Miles was our official leader, the four of us were the core who led the mission. We three felt Moon's compliments applied to us as well. Here, as almost everywhere in the organization, leadership was taken by a handful according to principles that were only implicitly understood.

"You are rich," said Moon, moving his hand in a semicircle, indicating the room and presumably what lay beyond it. Our prosperity had truly impressed him.

"No, Master," replied Miles. "You are rich. All this is yours. For you."

Moon radiated more smiles.

He turned to Neil Salonen; the president had accompanied him on the tour. "You have much to learn from this group," said Moon. "I want you to visit here often, perhaps as often as once a week."

Salonen nodded. But he never returned to Upper Marlboro.

When he left, Moon bought five candles, paying for them with five $100 bills. It was an expansive gesture, but nothing more. The money would come right back to him.

As I said, Neil never came to visit, not even once. The rift between those of us in the Upper Marlboro group and the national headquarters grew wider. The situation was exacerbated by Elizabeth Burns, the object of my Vietnam flirtation, who was now completely rehabilitated and established as State Commander. No longer was she a humble follower; technically she was our boss. But in fact she had nothing much to do except to devise intrigues and make trouble. Elizabeth tried to force her will upon me. She had no real staff, no troops, only a corps of five neophytes who seemed always to have tummyaches and couldn't work. Meanwhile, she wanted to direct our operations, our people, and we resisted her.

We did the same to Neil and headquarters. By now the 100-day training program, which was essentially what Level III had become, had been set up in Belvedere. It was growing increasingly clear to us that the training was taking on a fanatical turn. Moon had brought over some of his Japanese troops to show us the way, first a core of twelve and then a flood of four hundred. He also brought over a number of

Europeans, including a large group of Germans. In Germany, too, he seemed to appeal to a right-wing fringe. The head of the Germans was a former Hitler Youth.

We were drawing in recruits at a good rate, but we were not turning them over to Belvedere for the 100-day training, as we were supposed to. These people would have been redistributed afterward, and we wanted to keep them with us. However, the church seemed consciously destructive of allegiances between members. Our refusal was resented and challenged in headquarters, and the rift grew worse in time. We were well on our way to becoming a splinter group. It was felt in Washington that we were building a separate empire. We were thinking and acting independently. It was as if a microcosmic reformation were taking place. We represented a softening, a liberalizing tendency, while the main group, far from even staying in the same place, was moving toward a harder line. We did not, however, in any sense repudiate Moon. We still believed he was the messiah and loved him. We blamed all our differences on his followers, who we believed were following his will imperfectly.

For the most part, Moon seemed oblivious to the frictions within his camp. He liked us, too, because we were such good money-makers. For over a year the candle sales were the main source of funds in the United States and we were the masterminds of that activity. We stood as independently as we did for as long as we did only because of this situation. Otherwise, we would have been broken down, demoted, retrained and reassigned, as was the *modus operandi* of the Unification Church.

At this time the big push was on mobile bus teams, a new kind of recruiting, fund-raising having gone well enough to make the payments on Belvedere and get us nearly everything else we needed. Each state was to have a team, which was to drive around getting people interested in coming to our centers for lectures, workshops, and so on. In addition, there were two international bus teams—sort of teams at large, for special drives and uses. These teams, moving around in luxurious $75,000 buses, were headed by a Las Vegas entertainer and by Zeigler, who was still a comer. Kirby Smith, who was moving up again after having been deposed as president, was mid-Atlantic Commander of the state bus teams.

Also at this time there were numerous rallies, some of them in preparation for Moon's 21-city speaking tour in the fall of 1973. (The number, twenty-one, as always, was significant, being what was hoped was the beginning of a geometric progression by sevens.) When our people mixed with these bus teams headed by Zeigler and his like, they would come back deeply upset. Often, following huge prayer meetings, full of bravado and bluster and an increasingly militaristic format—questions and then answers boomed out in unison—our people, particularly the women, would start crying. Increasingly we tried to protect our group from such abrasive contacts. If that was impossible, we spent hours soothing them afterwards.

Finally the ax, suspended over our heads for so long, fell. Miles, who had taken the brunt of the long battle with Washington, absorbed the blow. He was to report to Belvedere for the 100-day training and then reassignment to some other post. Bitterly, resentfully, he went. He had been in the church for six years and now he was going back to learn it all over again with the raw recruits. One might well wonder why he went. Perhaps he felt he had no alternative. One might also wonder what else a young man who had spent such a large part of his life following a messiah would do. Such a past would simply not fit gracefully on any job résumé. Furthermore, he was caught in a logical bind. If Moon was the messiah, then Miles had better do what was ordained, pleasant or not. If Moon wasn't the messiah, then Miles had to admit he had made a terrible mistake. Such mistakes are nearly impossible to admit. It was tantamount to saying he had been crazy for six years.

Miles' slot was left unfilled. We didn't know who was jockeying for the job out there, but since we were an oligarchy anyway, things went fine, from our point of view, Elsa, Jeffrey, and me running things. When Moon held his first of many state directors' meetings in Belvedere, I went, though I held no official position there. I got away with it and I even managed to pull off a coup and get appointed bus commander for the state. I got the job the same way nearly all jobs were gotten there: I showed I wanted it, I pushed and hustled and maneuvered. My motives were better than the usual ones, though. I wanted to stop the Upper Marlboro center from being effectively dismantled.

Now my rank was equal to Elizabeth's. I could stymie her even more effectively. I even went to Moon himself and told him about the trouble with Elizabeth. He listened patiently in the parents' room of the Upshur Street house.

"I know all about it," he said. "In the end you must let me deal with it. Meanwhile, you must obey me. My lieutenants can fight if they must, but God will forgive them on the last day if they obey me."

Jeffrey, Elsa, and I began making clandestine visits to Miles at Belvedere. The visits had to be secret because such a thing as friendship was regarded with suspicion. On the other hand, we didn't have to be particularly secretive—it was enough to be discreet—because in fact there was hardly any real friendship there, and people, seeing us walking on the grounds, were hardly likely to think we came up only to see Miles.

One day just as the three of us were getting out of the car in the parking lot, we heard this terrible racket, which first seemed incomprehensibly strange and was eventually perceived as a cacophony of human voices. We walked over and peered through a high hedge around the grounds. That weird sound was the Japanese, *praying*. They were outside, kneeling in a group, and shouting at the top of their lungs. "Kneeling" was perhaps an understatement, for they were doing so in the new Oriental style, which meant that their faces were sometimes plastered to the ground, their shoulders only inches from the turf, their buttocks turned to the sky. This was not the stained-glass posture of the knight paying homage to his liege lord and his God at once, dignified, down on one knee, his head up, his right hand on his sword, his eyes open and blazing fervently. This rather was the posture of complete submission of a subject who presented himself as an utter object, an unperceiving footstool or doormat that would be grateful even for the recognition of the Master's feet wiping themselves.

This was the new spirit brought by Moon's four hundred Japanese fanatics, who lived full-time at Belevedere now. On this visit Miles told us that the Japanese were no longer praying to God. They figured their efforts would be more efficacious if from then on they just prayed directly to Moon.

We would seek out Miles and walk with him around the well-tended grounds. During that first visit he looked like a humiliated wreck, but Miles was slowly recovering himself. The 100-day training was intense. The trainees rose early, prayed, did karate exercises and then spent the day in mind-numbing lectures on the *Divine Principle*. Then after that they would be driven out to sell candles in the street for several more hours. And this wasn't the same *Divine Principle* that Miss Kim had taught us, but rather the gospel according to Mr. Kim, the head of the Korean church, who, like so many important leaders, had come over to the new Rome. This Kim taught a *Divine Principle* about three times longer and more complicated, also with lots of bogus biology and mystical electronics, which must have passed for science among the peasants of the Korean congregation.

Nor were these lectures anything like a typical course taught by an urbane professor. Rather they were taught by monotonous rote, the old Korean prison-camp routine. You would go through the teachings quickly, say in three days, and then you would go through them again, and again, and again, for one hundred days.

Once we brought Miles' brother to see him. William had returned from North Dakota in very bad shape. They weren't ready for Moon's word out in God's country, and he had not gotten a single convert. It was through him that we found out that Moon had told the Pioneers, as these new missionaries were called, that it would be better to commit suicide than to fail. We told him not to do that, but to come stay with us. So another wrecked soul joined the haven at Upper Marlboro.

We had a reputation for holding the hard cases. Sometimes headquarters even sent them to us, and we straightened them out and sent them back. If nobody wanted them we found room for them. We had discovered that if we could keep these people for a few weeks they wouldn't leave us. That began to change, though, and for the first time we were losing members.

Larry Gonzalez went insane. He had always been a super-fanatic, but now he came up with a new theory of who Christ was. Like the Japanese, he decided he was going to pray directly to Moon. He was a bug-eyed, intense fellow who had a black belt in karate, and we wondered what would happen if he ever went berserk and got violent. Larry was a problem that we passed on. We sent him to another center down South and hoped a new situation might change him.

One day Barnie Sawyer, a brilliant but crazy weightlifter who went into glass-smashing rages, just disappeared. He took Normie, who built the masterpiece candles, with him. The two of them apparently just walked in, packed their gear and went out on the road and hitchhiked away. Nobody realized what had happened until they were gone. Such things never used to happen.

I continued to go to the monthly directors' meetings. These were attended by the state directors and by the commanders of the bus teams—the One World Crusaders, of which I was one. I now had a bus and a team of ten. The church was more bureaucratic by this time as well. The bus teams and the recruiting drive were working as well as the earlier fund-raising. Gone were the days of three years ago when the whole American branch would have rattled around loose in Belvedere. Now Moon's followers numbered five or six thousand, far below what he wanted and far below the hundreds of thousands he claimed in Japan and Korea. But he was telling us now that he had turned the corner in the United States, that soon he would be a household word. Maybe he already was. He was getting press, and he didn't mind whether it was good or bad as long as it was press. Now for the first time the term Moonie was being applied to us. The time would come when Moonies called themselves Moonies and liked it, but we still felt the term was derogatory, as indeed it was intended to be. People found us creepy and sinister.

In June Rob Sheppard drove me up to Belvedere in the tan Torino. We sped across the industrial clutter of the Baltimore outskirts and through the nicer parts of the Maryland and Delaware countryside. Eventually we hit the New Jersey Turnpike north. The late morning grew hot and I pulled down my tie and tossed my blue suit jacket in the back seat with our sleeping gear and clean clothes. The radio wailed on and the wind streaming in the open windows made our faces slightly numb.

Rob was another of those all-American boys who did so well in the Unification Church. He had a sort of Terry-and-the-Pirates profile, a square jaw, white-blond hair, a ruddy complexion. Moon seemed to favor good-looking people. He showed the Oriental's love of a good exterior. There was none of this nonsense from him about losing this world and gaining the next. Moon expected you to have a firm foot in both worlds.

Rob only nodded uncommunicatively when I tried to make

conversation, so we lapsed into silence. It was a boring stretch of road. I was well into a good yawn when suddenly the car lurched and then ground along the gravel of the shoulder. Rob had done it again! He pumped wildly at the brakes, his eyes wide now. The car rolled to a stop. He had a terrible habit of dozing at the wheel.

Rob emptied his lungs and took a deep breath: "Wow!"

I laughed nervously, and Rob smiled sheepishly.

Already his eyes were glued to the rearview mirror. A moment later he pulled smoothly into a space in the heavy Friday traffic. Rob was a good driver when he was awake. He seemed to be good at everything. He was an athlete, with a black belt in karate, a scholar who took an eighteen-credit load in an honors program at the University of Maryland, and a leader who headed up the Towson operation. His father worked for the CIA. Before Moon, Rob's spiritual outlet had been theosophy.

"You've been working too hard again."

Rob nodded, but this time he was alert.

"You want me to drive?"

"No, it's all right."

I knew he wouldn't. It would have been contrary to the dogma. I was in Abel's position and he was in Cain's. He was to serve me. So I crossed my arms and settled back.

I did not speak until we crossed the Tappan Zee Bridge: "Take exit eight. Then when you get to the Howard Johnson's, it's the second estate on the right."

From the serpentine driveway leading to the main house at Belvedere we saw a soothing vista of rolling green lawns and gray stone buildings. Now Moon, Hak Ja Han and his seven children lived down the way at East Meadow, which was hardly less splendid or costly, with its $600,000 price tag. Fund-raising was still going fine. While Rob parked the Torino amid the clutter of the other vehicles—most of the other commanders and directors flew in, but some lived close enough to drive—I took my sleeping bag and claimed one of the forty-five or so iron bunks in one of the carriage-house sleeping rooms. The days of sleeping on floors were also largely past. We had even installed bunks in Upper Marlboro.

Behind the garage a couple of the Japanese were washing a car. Several hundred of them lived in the worst conditions and slept practically stacked on the floor of the house behind the main building. (Someone had told me that the Japanese word for the United States was "heaven.")

In the distance a tractor mower droned. I walked with Rob past the empty swimming pool, regarded by the church as a useless frivolity which would never be filled. The 100-day trainees, Miles among them, were entering the fourth quarter of their full day of lectures. They would break off for karate training, eat dinner, then sell candles for four hours on the streets. But Miles, having once submitted to his demotion— and such willing submission carried great weight—had gained back enough points that he could cut classes. After all, by this time there was hardly a leader who had not suffered the same fate, some even more than once. Life with Moon was a perpetual coming and going.

Keeping an eye out for Miles, I talked to the other commanders and directors—there were one hundred of us, one each from each state—who were trickling in. I found that my stock had risen—not much, a few fractions of a point—since the first days of Miles' disgrace. It was a steady and reassuring trend. Although one seldom spoke of such matters directly, one could always sense exactly where one registered on the rank barometer.

Dinner was fried chicken, rice and a little salad, laid out on the four Formica cafeteria tables outside the carriage house and eaten off paper plates with plastic forks on the lawn. I drank pulpless lemonade out of a Dixie cup. Some girls from Upper Marlboro were working in the kitchen, and one, Linda, forced a few special pieces of chicken on me. Food and nourishment was her karma and she accepted her lowly work—as we all did—with great cheerfulness. After all, what was the difference between kitchen duty and selling candles?

I saw Miles picking his way through the hands, feet and plates on the ground. With his luminous gray-green eyes, large ears, pointed chin and hooked nose, Miles looked elfin when he was smiling, which he was. I put my plate aside and stood, prepared for the inevitable bear hug. In the days just after I lost my job heading the FLF I had found Miles neurotic and oppressive. Later I regarded him as my mentor. Now he was my brother and a friend in need.

I noticed that he had two or three followers in tow, members of the group of ten he had been elected to head. The concept of submission in a pecking order was quickly established. He sent them to fill a plate for him, and to get coffee for me. They could hardly take their eyes off him. They were fascinated, absorbed in the mystique of someone fallen from on high and back on the rise.

We were glad to see each other. But after the hellos were over, I saw his troubled look, his goblin look, come over him.

"Are things any better?"

"Well, it's nearer the end. And they're going to make me a state leader—not in Maryland, some other state."

"That's great, Miles. I knew they wouldn't hold you down."

He looked away. With his large, reddish hooked nose I might have imagined it was a good stiff drink he held in his hand. But it was lemonade he swished thoughtfully around in his mouth and swallowed.

"It means starting all over."

"That's life."

"That's certainly life in the Unification Church."

I remained silent. I could offer Miles all my personal sympathy, but when he offered me evidence of his slipping faith, I could not always respond.

Miles shook his head sadly. "You should see the people here—who they're recruiting now."

"Yes, I know."

"Storm troopers. Kamikazes. Empty eyes. Empty heads."

"Why are there so many of them now?"

"This is where he's going. We got a whiff of this in Japan. This is what he wants. The Japanese church, the Germans are his models now."

Again I was silent. I was surprised that Miles, who at his worst was arrogant and self-righteous but who was always intelligent, had become so openly cynical.

"You should see them in the war games," he went on. "A couple of weeks ago he set the Japs on the Germans. I saw a guy with a broken arm. Another had a separated collarbone. You couldn't count the bloody noses."

"What does Mr. Moon do?"

"Nothing."

"He doesn't understand. But he will. He has to."

Miles grimaced and blinked his luminous eyes.

After dinner we lingered on the lawn. I had a month's worth of gossip to impart. By the time I went to turn in I realized it was rather late. I went through the anteroom with its couch and chairs where the Englishmen hung out now. One cupped a joint to his mouth as I passed. About sixty of these Englishmen had paid their way over following a billboard ad campaign promising six weeks of graduate level seminars in America with lectures on religion, philosophy, ecology, just about everything. Well, the promised professors of this and that from here and there showed up, but only once a week, and the rest was straight Unification Church. They promptly rebelled, but the passage money was spent. So they stayed on, a curiously disenchanted island amid the fanatical devotees. One or two even converted.

I awoke to the creaking of bedsprings above me, and the growing murmur of voices. I could hear a shower running. It must be late, relatively speaking. Breakfast was at seven sharp.

I stumbled to a small bathroom and found the usual scene:

one guy in the shower, one on the toilet, and four others trying to shave. I edged in sideways and got my toothbrush under the cold-water tap. I had to shave without lifting my elbows. I skipped the shower; the hot water was out. I put on a clean white shirt and underwear and wore my blue suit that had hung at the end of the bunk on a wire hanger during the night.

After another institutional breakfast on the lawn—powdered scrambled eggs and two quick paper cups of coffee heavily laden with sugar and milk—I went to the living room of the main house, where I sat on the carpet. The room was perhaps thirty feet by sixty and would have been comfortable for maybe forty-five people. Already twice that number were kneeling, sitting yoga style or leaning against the walls, and another forty or fifty were still to arrive. Males took one side of the room and females the other. The men wore coats and ties and the women conservative dresses or skirts. The men had short hair and not one wore a moustache or a beard.

At eight sharp everyone stood and the sea of bodies parted. Moon and his translator, Mr. Kim this time, walked briskly to the end of the room, where the glass French doors overlooked the garden. Generally, Moon stood, but he also leaned, perched, and sometimes sat on the small couch there.

"Good morning." His accent was thick; the *r* sound was typically Oriental, slurred.

"Good morning, Father," came the reply, forceful and in unison.

Moon was wearing a tunic-like white shirt outside his black slacks. He looked starched and crisp, even in this relatively informal attire. Although it was hot and would get hotter in the packed room, we were not to unbutton our collars and loosen our ties. Moon had told us he put a pin through his knots so his ties would never slip a millimeter. This he had told us in one of those many talks, like the one he was to give this morning, that lasted sometimes four hours, or six, even eight, and on very rare occasions, like during the days around Christmas two years ago, twelve or sixteen hours. His mind ranged freely during these talks and there was scarcely an aspect of life the Master had not passed on. He enveloped us in these speeches.

Moon sometimes gave away his suits to his underlings. This was an honor and a mark of affection. It was also a signal that when he was away these favored people had his authority and stood in his place, literally in his clothes. Moreover, Moon practiced shamanistic magic. He believed people and events could be controlled through the unseen spirits that, for instance, inhabited clothing.

His translator, Mr. Kim, had not been so favored. (Kim was a common Korean name, and this was yet another Mr. Kim, unrelated to Miss Kim or to the head of the Korean church or to Moon's first disciple.) It was not necessary thus to favor him, however, for this Kim was always in the Master's presence. Kim wore the kind of Robert Hall suit that the state might issue a prisoner after his time was served. If many of Moon's followers now dressed in these cheap, badly cut suits, it was partly because they had very little personal money. Kim, like Moon's other translators, seemed like a being who had been totally taken over, who had no will of his own. He was solely a reflection of Moon, literally a puppet who talked and moved when his master jerked the strings.

A friend who spoke Korean once told me about overhearing an exchange: "I have to take a piss," said Kim. "Tough, I have to take a shit. Stay!" said Moon. He counseled strength in the face of all discomfort. All inconvenience was to be regarded as training for the harder, leaner days to come.

I felt a great warmth when my eyes rested on Moon. I regarded him as my spiritual father. I wanted to win his trust, and felt that to some extent I had. I was not afraid of him as some others had confided to me they were, possibly because they were afraid of their own fathers. Moon

was misunderstood. He wanted us to be creative and inter-
pretive in carrying out his word. He did not wish to be taken
literally. He did not ask blind obedience. He was not the
harsh autocrat some took him to be. That was why we had
done so well and had prospered at Upper Marlboro and why
he was so pleased with us. Being from another culture, he
did not realize how weird some of his followers seemed in
terms of their own American culture. But eventually he
would understand.

Kim was invited to say the morning prayer. He did so in
the voice of a Bible-belt evangelical preacher. This revival-
tent voice was surprising the first time you heard it coming
out of this small, subdued Oriental. But Kim had learned his
English at a fundamentalist seminary in Chicago, and that
was how he spoke it.

Moon stood stolidly now, giving an impression of contained power in his thick shoulders and arms. His hooded
eyes sparkled darkly and he seemed to me to be laughing
inwardly, at himself or at us. I fancied he had a great sense
of irony. This cryptic look seemed to say that all this might
be a game, a cosmic joke, his being the messiah and us his
followers. But then, look again. He seemed to say: *It is true.*

After Kim's prayer, Moon, speaking directly in his heavily
accented English, asked: "How many of you have dreamed
of me?"

More than two-thirds of the congregation held up their
hands, including myself. I had dreamed some days ago that
I was waiting in a room. Three men had entered and left.
The air was strangely charged, as if about to break into
flames. The third man was Moon. I decided when I awoke
that the first two, who had also been Koreans in the dream,
were Adam and Jesus.

"How many of you have seen me in visions?"

About a third held up their hands. I had never seen Moon
in a vision.

Moon taught that when you saw him in dreams or visions

you were approaching—like a mirror that was aligned at the correct angle—the proper relationship with God. Many of his converts said he had come to them in dreams before they had even heard of him, much less seen him in a photograph. There were two particularly startling instances of this, in two groups as far apart as Oregon and Denmark. Of course, what we called "real life" was to Moon a mere illusion. "You do not really see me here," he would say, "because I am not really here. I am truly in the presence of God, where there is no space or time."

Now the state representatives stood to report on their candle sales, or any other money-making schemes—Moon was always interested in anything, anything at all that worked— and the number of converts. We were always far behind in our quotas and in a constant state of guilt about it. Moon taught that the more people who were converted when the judgment came, the less severe would be the ensuing holocaust. And though we were always doing better, all in all we were failing him miserably.

When my turn came, I reported: "From May first to June first we produced seventy-two thousand candles at the factory. We have four new members and six more people say they are returning to study with us. Seven or eight more have said they are interested in our workshops."

Moon was sitting on the couch now, his elbows on his knees and his head cupped in his hands. He sought eye contact as Kim translated, and he smiled and nodded.

That morning Moon elaborated one of the finer points of his moral system. This was his principle of "heavenly deceit," which justified lying by those in a higher state of knowledge to those in a lower state.

"You know the story of Esau and Jacob," the revivalist voice of Kim explained. "They were twins, only Esau was the firstborn. Esau was a hairy man, and Jacob smooth-skinned." Moon held up one arm and paused while Kim caught up. The light emanated from behind through the doors. Kim, standing a little nearer to us, went on: "Their father, Isaac, was old and blind. Jacob put lamb's wool on his arms and went to his father. 'I am Esau,' he said. 'Bless me as the first-born.' 'I do not believe you,' said Isaac. But Jacob held out his arms for his father to feel and Isaac blessed him. In this way Jacob stole his brother's birthright.

"When Esau found out, he went to his father. 'But I have no blessing to give you,' said Isaac. 'The blessing is given.' Esau wanted to kill Jacob. And so Jacob fled. He went away for twenty-one years, and grew rich. Then he returned. But first he sent his wealth, his wives, children and livestock to Esau. Then Jacob came. And Esau said: 'When I look into your eyes I see the eyes of God.' This is the first time in history that Abel subdues Cain. And because Cain is subdued, Jesus can be born from Jacob's line.

"The messiah cannot work until the harmony between brother and brother, between Cain and Abel has been restored," said Moon, speaking of himself in the third person, as he often did. "He will be thwarted until the restored Cain serves his brother and obeys him. But the world is full of Cains. What must we do? Until the better times to come, we must trick Cain for his own benefit until his eyes are opened through this principle of heavenly deceit."

This was the first time I had heard Moon's explanation of "heavenly deceit" since the incident with Ian MacIntyre, the bright new Georgetown graduate who had argued with the head of the Korean church, Young Whi Kim, over some editorial changes in the coming definitive edition of the *Divine Principle*. What was it Kim had said? "When you don't understand it, then you know it's *heavenly logic*."

At lunch break I ran into Frank Lyons at the buffet table and sat with him while we ate our bologna sandwiches. We made desultory small talk, grudgingly on my part, because how could I trust him after he had denounced me for my "sexual obsessions"? But then how could I bear a grudge after so long? How many times since then had he been rebuilt, reborn, rewired, retrained, reprogrammed and reoriented? I wondered what he thought of me now.

When we returned, I was able to sit close to Moon. Closer was better. As a teacher, the Master was not the type to tolerate the bright kids sitting in the back of the class. He wanted the bright kids up front. He wanted them to fight to get up front. And the strongest would win. It was a simple world.

Mr. Choi, an erect, thin, dark Mongolian type who had a Hitler lock falling over his severe high forehead, was invited to pray, and he launched into a long Hegelian harangue. I always remembered him for the Miracle of the Rock. Probably almost everyone there had heard Choi (who was not related to Mrs. Choi, the medium) tell of his out-of-body experience, when he was praying with all those more conventional ministers back in Korea, outdoors. He had seen their prayers, mere wisps wafting up to heaven. His own, he saw, was like a strong, clear beam rising to God. They were on the wrong path. He must warn them. In his fury (he would relate this part in a fury, acting out how he had picked up the rock—it must have weighed five tons) and with divinely inspired strength, he hurled it at their feet. The right path was Moon's.

When Choi finished, Moon opened the session up to questions. I was sitting at his feet, and he seemed to me the epitome of powerful masculinity. At moments like this, the Belvedere living room was like a locker room, with Moon the coach who owned his players heart and soul.

Seeing Frank must have started the train of thought. Homosexuality, even the latent homosexuality that had troubled so many of the young men whom I had known in the church, seemed a great gap in Moon's teaching. I recalled his other teachings concerning sex. I knew why we were rigidly segregated by sexes in this room, that we were to abstain from intercourse or any sexual activity until marriage. I knew that our marriages now were to be arranged by Moon according to principles greater than our own selfish pleasures or inclinations. I even knew why, when a couple consummated their marriage, it was to be in the woman-above position the first three times. That was because we began with and moved on from the woman-dominated fallen state where Eve's seduction of Adam had left us.

But what of the person who was tormented by homosexual yearnings? Segregation of the sexes was obviously no answer. Was lifelong abstinence enough? Or was that even permissible, since we were instructed to marry and fructify? Were the yearnings by themselves sinful? I did not know. Moon had never spoken of such matters. Perhaps I should have paused at this point. Many such questions were not really questions, on clearer reflection. It was a waste of time to ask those kind. But now a host of related questions were unleashed upon me. I must have the benefit of the Master's thoughts.

"Father," I asked when he called on me, "what are we to do about the matter of homosexuality?"

I was conscious of a stunned silence around me. There was always a courteous silence after a question, but this was extreme, as if everyone had stopped breathing during the time lag for translating.

Here came the answer: "If it really gets to be a problem, you tell them to cut it off, barbecue it, put it in a shoebox and mail it to me."

He laughed and the room exploded into laughter.

Sex-obsessed Allen had done it again! All eyes were riveted on me, and I could read those expressions: "Oh, you jerk! Now he knows you're queer!"

I sat down, confused, humiliated, aghast. How had this happened? What had I done? The next question was totally unrelated to mine, and the subject of homosexuality appeared closed for good. But my thoughts raced on. I was oblivious until suddenly the session ended. The ranks parted, and Moon and Kim passed by. Everyone bowed. It used to be that Moon shook hands Western style, but now the Oriental bow was in vogue. At each meeting, the bows grew deeper and deeper.

At the next month's meeting something even worse happened. It was at Sunday service, which began as always at five A.M. I had slept badly and awoke even earlier than necessary that morning, so I got right in the front row. We began with the pledge, which was very like the traditional Apostle's Creed. As we recited it, I was conscious that all the other members around the country would be reciting it, too, in the parents' rooms of the various living establishments, the sanctified places where Mama and Papa Moon slept when they came to visit. Again, there was an aspect of shamanistic magic to this. Moon's power was literal: it leaked from him. Places where he slept, the objects he touched, the carefully selected plots of land he had visited and prayed at in each state, all contained him and forever after brought closer to God those who came there to meditate and pray.

Moon was not present for the service. He was upstairs, going through it with the "blessed" couples, whom he would marry in the future.

When Moon came down to talk to us, I often met his gaze— possibly because I was in the front row. His eyes sparkled and his serene beaming expression seemed meant in part especially for me. The wonderful circuit between us was complete. Then, while explaining one of the parables of obedience, that of Abraham, who is told by God to sacrifice his son Isaac, Moon motioned me to come to him. My first thought was that he would ask me to confess my sins. Although confession is not a ritual in the Unification Church as it is in Catholicism, it is employed at certain points—for instance, before one is married. I prepared myself. I prided myself on my candor and certainly I was humble enough.

Moon motioned me to kneel.

I did so in an attitude of prayer.

No, he told me with gestures, I was to get down on all fours.

When I did, I was looking out at the expectant congregation. I felt a jarring smack on my rear. Moon had kicked me. The congregation was puzzled. So was I.

"Would you follow me if I treated you like this?"

Aha! Now they understood the drift.

"Yes!"

"What?"

"Yes!" came the crashing reply. The clenched fists shot upward.

"What?"

This time the reply was a mighty roar.

I looked behind and up to see Moon cupping his hand to his ear. Then he smiled and nodded. He motioned me up and gave me a gentle push away. I sat back down. It was some time before I had the courage to look around. In the eyes I caught, I saw a certain smirking amusement. Was I contemptible? Or blessed? I did not know. The kick itself had not been hard enough to hurt.

Afterward I discussed the incident with Miles, who had been sitting near me that morning.

"He cast me in the role of Isaac," I told him. "It was an honor. The kick didn't hurt. We were only acting out the story."

"Don't be an idiot," Miles replied evenly, and he looked blankly into my eyes. Unable to read his thoughts, I glanced away.

"This afternoon you'll get a taste of the war games," said Miles as we walked through the cafeteria line. He smiled dreamily.

"Yes." I was not looking forward to them. About the only good thing you could say about the games was that it would be nice to get some exercise after two constrained days of sitting on the living-room carpet, packed like sardines, listening to Moon.

When the time came we went to the field behind the main house. In the middle of it was a large boulder Moon had dubbed Holy Rock. Now Moon stood on top of it. These games, he said, were to instill pride in victory and shame in defeat. About sixty of the American cadre would face an equal number of the Germans who were living here at Belvedere. Moon favored pitting nationalities against one another, and more often than not in a World War II lineup. Here we were again, Axis and Allies, Americans against Germans. This was not contradictory to Moon's goals. Nationalism was a stage on the way to world unity, the Master taught.

We lined up opposite the Germans. Characteristically, there was an inordinate number of tall blonds. At Moon's signal we were to grapple with our opposite number. The object of the game was brutally simple. Each of us was to drag our opponent behind the lines.

"Go."

I paired off with Herman Oster, the Germans' leader, the former Hitler Youth now in his mid-fifties, but still well built and muscular. I had been amused to learn that he had a communications fetish and back in Germany was in constant radio contact, even in his car, with his underlings. I used my lower center of gravity, my more powerful shoulders against him. Maybe I outweighed him. I pulled. I turned him around and pushed. It was no go. He turned me back around and pushed. His leaden eyes bulged. His cheeks turned crimson. Wordlessly we grunted and heaved, but neither of us could budge the other. After ten minutes we were still right on the line. This called for strategy. I would use psychic mastery. I sought eye contact. But his gray eyes blazed just as fiercely back. Suddenly I half crumpled, as if something—my will, my back— had snapped. In that instant of surprise, before he could exploit the apparent advantage, I dropped low and got his ankle. I yanked and he went down. The rest was easy. I dragged him quickly and efficiently behind our line. His arms flailed uselessly, unable to find a countergrip.

I had been just too wrought up to lose. Oster was crestfallen. He hunched his shoulders, hung his hands, stared at the ground. But soon he was jubilant. All in all, the Germans were winning. I could care less. I felt no shame in defeat. And my victory, I felt, was personal. I had outfanaticked a fanatic.

Something strange was hapening at Upper Marlboro. I was falling in love with Elsa. Now it seemed as if I had always been in love with her. I recalled how she had nursed me, some three years ago, the week I had been so sick just before I was appointed to head the FLF. Small, dark haired and fair skinned, delicate and fine boned, Elsa was often unobtrusive and withdrawn, but always a force of leadership. One had a tendency to overlook Elsa. She worked hard, gave the benefit of her fine intellect and asked very little in return, certainly nothing like official position, which in fact she did not hold. Yet at Upper Marlboro her talents and maturity—she was thirty, five years older than I—had raised her to the level of a sort of straw boss. As I looked back over the several years that I had associated with Elsa, I realized what a wonderful person she was.

Elsa had a unique background among us. She was at least a second-generation cult member. Her parents had been followers of Eberhardt Arnold, a philosopher and theologian who had died in Germany in the Thirties. The group was philosophically related to the Anabaptists and, among other things, they were pacifists. Because of this, mainly, the group was forced to leave Germany as Hitler rose to power. They went to England, but when the war broke out, they faced internment. They decided to leave England, but no other country seemed likely to take them. They wrote dozens, perhaps even a hundred countries, seeking to immigrate, but no one would have them, except one they were not likely to have chosen. Paraguay needed settlers and they went. After the war the members of the Arnold cult, called the Society of Brothers, came to the United States, where no doubt they felt more at home. Other Anabaptists in the nineteenth century had settled in Canada and the far Western states: Washington, Wyoming, Idaho and Montana. Elsa's parents' group settled, however, in Farmington, Pennsylvania.

The Brethren lived a simple Christian communal life there, farming and making handcrafts, including sturdy, simple, beautiful wooden toys. They continued to speak their native German, as well as the two languages of their recent odyssey, English and Spanish. That was how Elsa came to speak those three languages.

Some months earlier, Elsa's father had died. She had gone up to Pennsylvania to be with him the week that he had succumbed to cancer. His death had been lingering and painful and yet, because of his beliefs and the strength of his character, peaceful. When Elsa came back from that trip, I met her at the airport, and I sensed that she was changed. The Brethren believed that Moon was the Antichrist, the false prophet who precedes the real messiah, according to Revelations. He would win wars, unite religions even, but in the end he would oppose the real messiah and lose. Others had leveled this Antichrist charge at Moon, and he spent a fair amount of time implicitly refuting it in his teaching and lecturing. The Brethren thought religious beliefs were entirely a matter of individual conscience and they would not put pressure on one of their own daughters, even. Yet I sensed that in witnessing the death of her father in that community, Elsa had had some kind of experience that had brought her nearer to them, if not back to them, spiritually.

Elsa threw herself into her work. She hid out in the candle factory, working all hours and exhausting herself. She did not come to our Sunday morning services. I suspected she had lost faith in Moon. She was with us now only out of personal loyalty.

In the first weeks of our attraction I inevitably recalled my flirtation with Elizabeth Burns. It had been innocent, not much more than seventh-grade hand-holding, and yet it had caused me much trouble, both at the time when I was relieved from the FLF post, and later, when I suffered a terrible backlash from Elizabeth. Would this be the same?

Yet for all my worries I knew there was something right about my attraction for Elsa. My feelings for her were sincere and natural, as indeed had been my sentiments for Elizabeth. But with Elsa my feelings ran deeper, and things had changed, both with me and my circumstances. Elsa and I were craftier, for one thing, and we hid our special regard for one another. At night, after everyone else had gone to bed, we met and talked. This was the conversation of lovers. We went over the events of the day, testing our perceptions on each other, balancing things out, cross-reading personalities and happenings, learning from one another. It was just the kind of relationship Moon sought to extinguish in his followers and which he explicitly forbade between the sexes. Love, when it is allowed to flourish between two thinking beings, brings a heightened perception of value. It is a blissful state. To us, it represented a gradual return to sanity.

The people who came to Moon were almost universally confused about sex, and that really meant they were confused about love. Most of them, undoubtedly including myself, wanted to escape, at least for a time, from combat in the erogenous zones. My sexual experience with Flo, which immediately preceded my entering the Unification Church, had exhausted and discouraged me. I suspect that seeking such escape is at times the sanest thing to do, and, furthermore, that it is often a good part of the impulse to join the Catholic clergy, for instance, which is generally considered a sane and productive thing to do. But Moon channeled this escape impulse in such a way as to hold people in perpetual thrall. In the crudest sense, he seized control of our sexuality at a time when we were inclined to relinquish it. He forbade any kind of sexual interaction, sublimated or not, until he chose our spouses, making himself in a very real sense the center of each follower's sex life.*

But Elsa and I, in communicating this way, were breaking the spell. Although we hardly knew it at the time, we must have been crossing the fairy ring that Moon had drawn around us to hold us. Our romance was a gentle pre-sixties love— meaning we did not go to bed. It was sweet and chaste, a delightful experience missed by many of our generation, who were more likely to wake up in bed after a night in a singles bar and not know each other's names. It was not the stressful sort of relationship I had had with Flo. Before we realized how far we had drifted from Moon we used to imagine that

---

* Moon may have once been the center of his United Family members' sex lives in quite another sense, according to an unpublished paper written by Yun Ho Ye at Princeton Seminary in 1959. This Korean minister cites evidence that when Moon founded his Tong-Yil-Kyo sect, as it is called in Korea, he and his followers practiced a sort of messianic pansexuality, though in secrecy. Moon was initiated into the free-love cult by a woman, aged fifty, in 1946, Duek Eun Chung, whom he then regarded as his divine mother: Chung later confessed this after having a revelation, according to Ye, who cites published sources. According to Ye, when witnesses revealed his cult's secret promiscuity, Moon was imprisoned on the grounds that it was destructive to the family and injurious to public morals. Imprisoned in Pyongyang, Moon met Il Duk Kim and his wife, who also believed in promiscuity. Moon continued to dogmatize promiscuity with Chung after he was released, Ye says, and he was arrested and imprisoned again, this time in Houng-Nam. Ye quotes from the purported confession of an early Moon follower who said that when Moon was forty "the present world will be ended through the Third World War," though the end might be postponed six years if Moon's goals were not realized by then, which would have been approximately 1960. "By that time," according to the confession, "Moon becomes the Divine Father of 210 women; that is, he must have sexual relations with 70 virgins, 70 widows and 70 men's wives. The 210 women will develop to 144,000 spiritual people. These people will be saved from the war."

he might marry us. Miss Kim, who was virtually the only person we could confide in, gave us hope that if she put in a word for us he might make an exception and honor our desires.

At some point, though, we realized that we were drifting, even if we didn't fully understand how far. My parents had bought a house in Mexico, down in San Cristóbal de las Casas, one hundred miles northwest of the Guatemalan border. We were invited to visit there if we wished; the house was empty. Gradually my relations with my parents seemed to have been improving. At least there was no more banshee screaming from my mother. And my father had preserved his noncommittal do-as-you-must attitude, even when once I brought mind-reading Mona by and she told him with the coquettishness of a flouncing walrus that she had met him years ago during an astral trip. Gradually I had started going home more and sometimes my father and I even played chess, which was abstract enough. That was another sign that I was coming down out of an orbit I had been in for over four years.

We were generally discouraged from seeing our families, but never forcibly restrained. Force wasn't necessary. If you believed Moon's teachings you believed that the rest of the world was in the hands of Satan. You were told that your family members were your enemies and that you could expect them to try to bring you back to the old evil ways. It was a catch-22 mode of thinking. The more your family tried to win you back, the more they proved that Moon was right and the more desperately you resisted. It was catch-22, because if you were sane they were crazy, and if you were crazy they were sane, but if you were crazy you weren't about to concede they were sane.

Miss Kim had explained to me about my family long ago— in her own gentle way—and it worked perfectly. In the more than four years that had passed since then, the doctrine and method of handling families had been refined, perfected, firmed up, made more explicit, like many of Moon's teachings. If at first he groped his way along a dark footpath, moving by uncanny intuition toward whatever worked—he was always the most pragmatic of religious leaders—later he would ride there on a brightly lit highway. His psychological efficiency was ever improving.

When we did visit our families, it was almost always with other church members, so we could resist collectively and make sure one of our people didn't waver during a period of vulnerability and doubt. Sometimes we even had reasons for wanting to visit someone's family; they might have something we wanted—especially money. Wealthy, influential families tended to get more visits than no-account, poor ones.

While sometimes I saw my family alone, I often visited them with others—besides Mona, Miles, who had particularly disliked them. They were crimson Satanists to him; they probably excited his envy or reminded him of his own shortcomings or ambitions or possibly some mixture of these things. That had been during the period when I had found Miles so domineering.

"Let's go to Mexico," Elsa said impulsively one day. A few months before it would have been unthinkable.

Elsa and I and Jeffrey scraped up whatever personal money we had and went. Elsa had the most money, since she had a tax refund from the Columbia Heights day-care center, which she had returned to after she came back from Colorado. We drove off in one of the communal cars. We picked up Miles on the way to Mexico. By now he had been rebuilt, had finished his 100 days and had been reassigned to head the Louisiana center in New Orleans.

We stopped over in Chesterville, Virginia, and I called my old professor, John Bessin, who was teaching there. Bessin put us up for the night. He was divorced from Margaret, who presumably was still a searcher somewhere else, without him or the two boys, of whom John had custody. John seemed happy and fulfilled, even without his wife. He told me that he had tried to hold her but simply couldn't. John was about forty by this time, and he'd gotten the big degree, his doctorate, and was teaching the kind of courses in archetypal myth and C. G. Jung that he had always wanted to teach.

He ribbed me about being a bit overweight, which I was. Stress tended to send me on eating binges, and I was now in a condition that my grandmother had called, the last time she had seen me, apostolic bloat. I filled John in about the last years in my life, about which he had been in the dark. There was something unshakably academic in John, and he kept referring to Moon as "Doctor" Moon. He filled me in, too. Chuck Martin, he said, had gotten married, but his wife had made it a condition that he give up communism, which he had.

But the real surprise was Bill Galen, who was living with Bessin. Bill, the former head of SDS at Sewanee, had run off a cliff in a car in April 1968, just days before his graduation. The car had been driven by a kid I remembered as the one who had dragged a dead pigeon around on a string everywhere he went for three weeks. Bill suffered a severe concussion, the effect of which was memory loss. He had slowly recovered from the damage, and was now, as far as I could tell, as acute as he'd ever been.

That night we all smoked dope, drank a lot of red wine, listened to raunchy music until very late and talked. Bill seemed such a sweet soul, kind and good. Through him I recollected all that had seemed wild and passionate about those college years. His story struck me as particularly poignant. I was reminded that there were many ways to blow apart and lose your faculties and I felt that in some strange way Bill's experience paralleled my own. Like me, he seemed to be coming out of an enchantment that had lasted all those years. For a moment, high on marijuana, I wondered if every twenty-five-year-old in America had somehow gone through the same thing in different ways.

After Atlanta we drove west and then south to Brownsville, Texas. We went over the crest of the Sierra Madre and over the central plateau into Mexico City. For Elsa, in a way, this was traveling a road previously not taken, because she once had been offered an archeological scholarship to the University of Mexico. For Miles, the fact that the people around him spoke Spanish, which he did not, was a constant irritation. He was even irritated that Elsa and I spoke Spanish, because he was reduced to the role of a dependent. Domineering Miles, who had gone so far as to order my meals and pick my clothes, could hardly find his way to a bathroom without my help.

Mexico was another world, and because of that, it was good for us. Even the air was different—dusty, palpable, spicy-smelling. For tourists, Mexico is ruins, museums, Mayas, other Indians, old and different religions. This land, it seemed, was ruled by different gods. We went through tunnels, took pictures on top of pyramids with the Pentax Jeffrey had brought, toured an ancient temple of the moon, and visited the beautiful anthropological museum in Mexico City, which had the poetry of men who had lived millennia before Christ inscribed on the walls.

We drove south, through Oaxaca, by which time we had been in Mexico seven days. We phoned Upper Marlboro and were told by Arthur Wilson, whom we had left in charge, that Washington had whiffed something irregular and was calling every day. Each time, Arthur told us, he made an excuse that I or Elsa or Jeffrey was out on some errand. We drove further south, where the sun beat down so hard we had to wear straw hats whenever we were outside. We slowly traveled higher and further south until at last we came to San Cristóbal on a plateau seven thousand feet high and surrounded by an almost perfect circle of higher mountains. My parents had a house overlooking this valley and when we awoke in the morning we had spiced strong Mexican coffee out on a terrace where we could see the mist burning off the valley and hear the quiet broken by the crowing of cocks and the gobbling of turkeys. Although we were not far from the equator, we were high enough so that we needed a roaring fire in the living-room fireplace at night.

We phoned Arthur again and found that headquarters was still breathing down our necks. They were sending Willard Zeigler on a fact-finding mission to Upper Marlboro. We told Arthur to make him comfortable and started home. At Vera Cruz we put Jeffrey on a plane back. He was the business manager, and he could hold things together until the rest of us returned.

It was on that long drive back that the spell was utterly and finally lifted from my shoulders. It came as it went, without my being fully conscious of what was going on. This journey was part of it, of course. It was as if we had chosen to take a literal trip to parallel the mental one Elsa and I had embarked on back in Upper Marlboro. At first I was inclined to give C. S. Lewis too much credit. I was riding in the back seat of the car and reading *That Hideous Strength*, the last volume of his science-fiction trilogy. (We were all great readers of science fiction at Upper Marlboro. That summer *Dune* had amounted to a cult book. Our favorite television program was *Star Trek*.) The villains of the book were members of a great benevolent-seeming science-oriented society who purported to want to better all mankind but really were intent on strangling everything that was human, vital and valuable. Suddenly I saw how much like Lewis's pompous meanies the Moonies were. The book struck a deep emotional chord, and I laughed and chortled as we drove back, choked until tears rolled down my face. When I finished the book, I knew I was out of the Moonies.

Elsa was already effectively out, but Miles was having a

much harder wrestle with his demons. He had doubted longer than I had, but he was an embittered personality, and he could not let go of those six years he had put in. All the rest of the drive we argued matters out with Miles. He was trying to do something that was fairly common with people in his situation.

"If Moon isn't the messiah," argued Miles, "then he is Satan. That means we ought to dedicate our lives to Jesus."

I told Miles that all he was trying to do in switching the good and evil roles around like this was trying to hold on to the whole system. I urged him not to try to keep his system intact.

"We don't know who Moon is," I said. "God knows who Jesus was."

Miles was still floating when we dropped him off in New Orleans. But he did know he was packing up his gear and coming to Upper Marlboro to live, without official permission.

When we arrived at Upper Marlboro Zeigler was installed in the best bed, a big antique that had come with the house. Again he began a campaign of conquest with the bed. Zeigler told Elsa and me that it was the Master's wish that we go to the 100-day training where we would be broken down, disassembled and rewired for duty at some other post. We told Willard, with all due respect, that we didn't think we'd be going. He said that he was empowered by the Master to take control of Upper Marlboro. Then we hit him with the shocker. We had incorporated Upper Marlboro, actually had done it under orders of headquarters, which was now employing some legal talent. However, this time they had outsmarted themselves. The separate incorporations were intended to keep the church from being financially wiped out by a big lawsuit for damages, such as some parents had been threatening. Now we ordered Zeigler off the property we legally owned.

But before he went we held a meeting of all our people in the big living room. Jeffrey, Elsa, Miles, and I, who had quickly flown up from Louisiana, told our membership, which had been whittled down now to about twenty-seven by various projects, that we no longer believed in Moon but that we were holding on to Upper Marlboro. They could go with Zeigler or stay.

Willard addressed the meeting. A relationship with God was possible only through Moon, he said. Although he took a long time, essentially he said that those who stayed with us were in the hands of Satan and going to hell. Then we spoke. What we said—that God could reach us all individually and separately—came as a surprise to the membership, because we had hidden our spiritual confusion. What happened next explained a great deal of what had been going on at Upper Marlboro all along. One guy went with Zeigler and all the rest stayed. We had developed a group loyalty greater than anyone's individual loyalty to Moon, except for the one fellow who couldn't break away. We were a genuine splinter group, an absolute heresy.

Now the question was, what were we going to do with ourselves. Although we began to feel we were freed from some kind of evil spell, it was not an altogether happy thing. We did not celebrate and kick up our heels. Within a few days we realized we were living in a fearful limbo. To some extent we were living in the very condition of existence we had sought to escape by joining up. We were face to face with the existential realities of life and it was scary. There was a cold winter wind blowing outside.

We huddled together. At times we were in a defiant mood. We smoked big black cigars, drank jug wine and lounged around reading *The Hobbit* out loud. We played cards until the early morning. We watched *Kung Fu* on the tube while Rob Sheppard critiqued the karate. We decided we would sell the place and give the money to the Communist Party. All witnessing, all candle-making, all the million little schemes, workshops, propagandizing, and projects that kept us busy, busy, busy, kept us from facing whatever it was we were afraid to face—all that stopped.

Another time we decided we'd like to give the place to Miss Kim. Jeffrey, who was tuned into the technological and ecological prophets, people like Buckminster Fuller, wanted to stay together and go down to Baja California and build a clean nuclear reactor or something.

Meanwhile the phone was ringing and visitors were knocking. Emissaries of the Master were on the horn. He was in Detroit, wanted us to come and see him. They were sure he would forgive us. In fact, the word was he already had forgiven us. Colonel Pak called and assured us we would be given jobs of even higher responsibility if we just submitted to the 100-day cerebral scrubbing.

One of Moon's three mediums, Mrs. Pai, arrived with her teenage daughter Hak Bon, who was fluent in English. Mrs. Pai brought good messages from the spirit world and a big bag of groceries: we were going to have a feast. We turned her down. She sat on the living-room floor and started giving her testimonial. It was a good one, but we had all heard it many times before. She was an intriguing woman and, among other things, performed exorcisms. She'd done something involving chickens, blood and candles to one poor fellow plagued by homosexual demons, but it hadn't been effective for long. I told Hak Bon to stop translating. Then most of us went upstairs and watched a television sci-fi movie.

Elsa took a group up to the Society of Brothers in Pennsylvania, where her mother still lived and her brother was a minister, which they called a Servant of the Word. At this point this group made a great impression on most of us. The Brethren were gentle, peaceful, low-keyed. They claimed to have no special lever to bring God's blessings. Yet they seemed genuine seekers, genuine lovers of their neighbors. How antithetical this was to the ways of the Moonies.

And yet the Brethren offered themselves as a buffer against the cold existential bath of the real world. They welcomed us, if we wished to come and work and meditate and discuss. There was no such thing as *joining* them, however. They resisted the very concept. I remember coming back from the visit by car during a snowstorm. No one spoke for hours, and the snow had silenced almost everything outside.

That Christmas I went home for the holidays, taking, however, an entourage from Upper Marlboro: Jeffrey and Miles, as well as Elsa, whom I told my parents I was going to marry. Although things had been getting better between me and my parents, I suspect that I took my friends because I was afraid to be alone with them for too long. Even so, uncomfortable scenes did transpire.

Perhaps my parents were afraid to be alone with me, too. "What are you looking so happy about?" my father asked me one evening when they had guests for cocktails. I had not been aware of his presence. He had sidled up beside me and caught me off guard. Had I actually been looking so happy? At any rate, I realized that in my father's view I was a poor stiff who had woken up and found four and a half years of his life gone.

Jeffrey got along well with my parents; he spoke their lingo. He was a charming fellow. Elsa did well enough, too, though the situation was much harder for her. She put up with some needling from my father, and even summoned a little wit in an uncomfortable situation.

"What do you think of Allen?" he asked flat out at the dinner table one night.

"Oh," she said, blushing. "Well . . . he is a little too *fat.*"

That brought a round of laughter and ended the ostensibly friendly line of questioning.

Miles had a terrible time. He thought my parents were awful people. What he really wanted to say was that they were in the hands of Satan, except that we didn't work for Moon anymore. Miles was having the hardest time coming down, abandoning a mode of thinking that had served him for so long.

The worst thing for me to get through, though, was when Flo came over for dinner. Inevitably, the sight of her took me back. I remembered lunches on the university green so many summers ago. I remembered how I had been frightened by her questions about my future.

Flo had not escaped that wave either. She had not even—no more than I—gotten her bachelor's degree yet. She had not married a good citizen with a law degree and gone on to raise children in a house with a pool and a piano. Although she had seemed practical compared to me, Flo had drifted through the years during which I had lost track of her. She had hitched around the country for a year and ended up spending a lot of time in Colorado, I think, though I can't remember for what reason. I know she lived in a commune for a while. I know she told me about driving a cab in Boston for a year, too, with a black Labrador retriever who always sat on the seat beside her. Her drift had also taken her spiritually eastward. Most recently she had been down in Florida studying Kundalini yoga with Yogi Blayan, who was the foremost teacher in the United States of this path, which involved blood-cleansing, firebreathing, and tantric practice. Hot stuff, but she had left it, not because she had found some fallacy, but rather because she had felt herself losing her Western ego-consciousness.

When Flo walked in the door I met another Allen, the one who might have stayed with her, the one I had run away from. The Allen who would go back to Upper Marlboro had taken another fork in the road. I was confused by this double image of myself. I could not bring myself to tell her I was marrying Elsa. That was a bad sign. It seemed as if Flo and I had some unfinished business to attend to. My solution, however, was not to face the situation or to force a resolution. I would try, after that one tantalizing evening, to forget that Flo existed.

I returned to Upper Marlboro, where the phones had stopped ringing and where the emissaries of Moon had stopped knocking. Headquarters was taking another tack. They were suing us for the property.

We got a lawyer. He was eager to go to court. We had a perfect case and he was keen to deal a blow to Moon's weirdos. When we did get to court, however, we found out that we were in for a long civil suit. We went back and got out our cigars, our wine, our cards, but it soon became clear that we were not going to be able to stick it out here for the years it would take to resolve the suit. We began to think of settling out of court.

Various pressures were pulling our group—down to a dozen or so now—this way and that. Many members, including Jeffrey, were being drawn into the Brethren. Elsa and I were going ahead with our wedding plans. We were to be married at Hodge Road by the mayor of Princeton, but those plans were quickly changed by a phone call from my father.

My mother wasn't going to be able to go through with it, my father said. She was either really sick or having an anxiety attack.

"You understand, don't you, Allen? You understand that my first duty is to my bride?" my father asked.

Elsa and I were married at Upper Marlboro by a minister wearing an electric-blue suit. We took one of the communal cars as a wedding gift (fair enough, since Elsa had donated her personal car years ago) and went down to San Cristóbal for our honeymoon.

By the time we got back it was obvious that the group would have to settle out of court. We simply had to rejoin society, whether it meant going back to school, getting a job or going to the Brethren, where a number had gone and more were going to go. Jeffrey was getting married to Jennifer, a girl in the group, and going up himself.

When we finally settled out of court, the house and property in Upper Marlboro were sold to a third party. The candle factory was sold to a man from the Eastern Shore of Maryland. So, the national Unification Church in the end was unable to steal from us the fruit of labors that we had done in the name of God.

Elsa and I headed for the University of Dallas, where my grandmother, Caroline Gordon, was teaching writing and where my sister (her namesake) was studying. My sister Caroline was then in her early twenties.

The University of Dallas came well recommended. I majored in English literature but was unable to throw myself back into academic life. Although I enjoyed my classes, I entertained a great deal of free-floating anxiety about my capacity to perform as a breadwinner after college, for my wife and potential children. My wife and I decided to leave Texas and go to the Society of Brothers. I worked for some months making toys there, but soon I grew discontent and was drawn to the outside world. My daughter was born at the community, and my marriage was buried there—another story in itself.

I returned to Princeton and got a number of pickup jobs, none of which lasted. I house-sat for my parents and friends. I was an orderly at my father's clinic. I worked in a phone boiler room conducting polls and surveys—on soaps, dog food, politicians, nuclear reactors, any products—with housewives and elderly ladies. I went back to school—and dropped out again.

And I picked up again with Flo. That situation did not take long to resolve itself for the worse. Somehow Flo was just as she had been before. She was working as a secretary in Princeton and living at home. Yet after all we had been through she was still telling me to balance my checkbook. When I told her I had dropped out of school, she called up the registrar and put me back in, but I dropped out once again.

McCarthy ran for president again that year, 1976, as a third-party candidate. My mother was his vice-presidential candidate in New Jersey, and I voted for her.

One day when McCarthy was giving a speech at Rutgers, Mom, Flo, and I went together. It seemed that the cycle was complete, and there we all were, returned to a point of origin.

Epilogue

In the Land of Nod

HERE AT THE END I FIND MYSELF WANTING TO REFLECT a little bit about my dark odyssey. From a distance of five years Moon's *New Heaven and New Earth* seem more like *The Island of Dr. Moreau* than a restored Garden of Eden. When I began working on setting down my experiences with Jack Vitek, I discovered with him that a simple narrative approach would allow us to tell the story without a lot of moralizing to predispose the reader. Now that we have rendered the story, I can't resist naming my experience, sharing some of the insights I have brought back with me from my strange sojourn.

In the late sixties and early seventies the two great symbols of American civilization—political freedom and economic prosperity—lost their constellating power. The psychological and moral confusion unleashed by the prosecution of the war in Vietnam has yet to run its course. Richard Nixon's Machiavellian abuse of the highest office in the land received "divine" sanction, when Jerry Ford pardoned the culprit and obviated the impeachment process. The dissonance in the signals coming from high places, the "credibility gap," the loss of faith in constituted authority, the systematic murder of hundreds of thousands of Vietnamese peasants: these things are bearing fruit today. In the face of our political leaders' inability to assert moral authority we are confronted with the rise of absolutist religious cults led by men whose claims to absolute moral supremacy go unquestioned by their followers. I once told a leader of one of Mr. Moon's International One World Crusade bus teams that I thought it was possible for God to inspire me independently of Mr. Moon. He replied, "Allen, that is not the *Divine Principle*. You are taking a Satanic position."

What does a cult follower gain? All the questions surrounding growing up—like what profession to choose, coming to terms with one's sexual orientation, where to live, how to find friends who share one's concerns, how to establish emotional independence from one's parents, whom to vote for in the next election—are precluded. Existential anxiety, which so often becomes acute in the late teens and early twenties for many Americans, is drastically reduced if not totally extinguished by membership in a cult. The cult member receives a new identity based on his or her relationship to the cult leader and predicated on absolute acceptance of his religious ideology. Status is based on one's ability to articulate the cult ideology and to implement its goals. And here, as in business, nothing succeeds like success.

In the Unification Church the power to produce is taken as a direct sign of God's blessing. If one's entry into the Unification Church moves apace, one's former life recedes into insignificance except as evidence for God's infinite love in having beaten you about in a special way so that you could recognize the truth after having it drilled into your head for seven or twenty-five or forty or one hundred days, depending on what kind of mission God has in store for you. It is a curious paradox that an independent or semi-independent decision of conscience can become the foundation for the grossest form of moral slavery. Implicit in accepting Moon's divine spider web is the notion that people who don't know his ways are morally blind. In other words, when a normal citizen tries to make a decision about what's right and wrong, at worst he has committed an act of hubris, at best an impotent, well-meaning act of moral solipsism.

To have discovered the absolute truth is a wonderful experience. Talk about getting high—Moonies who see the light are often among the highest people in the world. Whether or not the truth is *true* is up for grabs, but the experience of having found it is real. And there is nothing quite like it. Tears of relief, gratitude, and love come forth; finally, the reasons for all the failure, fear, confusion, misfortune have been made clear. In fact, they were worth it, because in those dark hours I was unconsciously paying for my ticket to the promised land.

Another paradox the Moonies live out is that while they have accepted the notion that, apart from Moon, they are incapable of making accurate moral judgments or even existential life decisions, they are perfectly competent to judge those outside the fold. This situation reminds me of the passage in Genesis where Lucifer holds up the apple to Adam and Eve and says take this and eat it. It will make you wise like God, knowing both good and evil. I'm no deep student of history, but it seems to me from my reading that the worst fanatics have been those who have had such a python grip on the absolute truth that they were compelled to administer it to their heathen brothers.

Moon readily lends himself to comparisons with other famous demagogues of the twentieth century, but when I think about him my mind is irresistibly led back to ancient Egypt, in which religious absolutism reached an apex in the worship of death . . . life serving death. If I try to look at him in American terms, I think of him as Asia's revenge for all those

Protestant missionaries we unloaded over there in the nineteenth century, while we were checking out the raw materials. He's a kind of bastard son of monopoly capitalism and a fierce Protestant fundamentalism.

Since I left the Unification Church, I have helped about ten people to see their way out of it. Since August of 1978 I have been working as a counselor for cult-related problems. I made the decision to do this work after attending a conference of parents of cult members and ex-cult members, along with a number of doctors, lawyers and members of the clergy. I attended the conference, which was held in Baltimore, with my friend (an ex-Moonie) Steve Hassan in the middle of August. Looking at the anguish on the faces of the parents who had lost a child to a cult moved me more than anything I ever experienced in the Unification Church. I had given four and a half years of my life to Moon. Lost years, or so it had seemed. Now I realized that the experience of those years could be put to good use. I could perform a real service for many people all over the country and at the same time begin to save money for graduate school in psychology.

In 1975, before becoming actively involved in helping kids get out of cults, I wrote a short autobiographical article about my experiences called "My Four and a Half Years With the Lord of the Flies." This article has been circulated all over the country by deprogrammers, parents of Moonies, and ex-Moonies. Because of this article I have been invited to assist in many deprogrammings. In most cases I declined, because in good conscience I could not condone the use of force or restraint. With one exception, all the Moonies I have talked to were completely unrestrained. In fact, I now make it a condition that for parents to hire me, they must have the express consent of their child in the cult.

Doing this work is fascinating, deeply satisfying, sometimes frightening, and always exhausting. People often ask me whether I fear reprisals from the Moon organization. I generally reply by saying, "Well, I don't think about it." But the fact is that I know that their teaching does not preclude violence. In November of 1978 a mother of a Moonie showed me a letter that her son (a member for three years) had sent her. In the letter he said that if she made trouble for the Church either she, his father, or her sister might have to die.

Each case I have worked on is unique. There are some common variables. If I had to reduce what I do to a few words, it would boil down to something like trying to convince young men and women that they can work, they can fight for righteousness, they can make a difference, they needn't prostrate themselves before some divine king in order to be justified. I invite them to leave Eden, to come back onto the field of battle, to enter a world of uncertainty where knowledge of the truth does not exempt them from moral responsibility, a world where their successes and failures will be their own.